FOSSILS

OF

NEW ZEALAND

HAMISH CAMPBELL, ALAN BEU, JAMES CRAMPTON, LIZ KENNEDY AND MARIANNA TEREZOW

WHITE CLOUD BOOKS

This print published in 2023 by White Cloud Books, an imprint of Upstart Press Ltd.
First published in 2013 by New Holland Publishers (NZ) Ltd

Upstart Press Ltd.
26 Greenpark Road, Penrose, Auckaland 1061, New Zealand

www.upstartpress.co.nz

Copyright © 2013 in text: GNS Science
Copyright © 2013 in photography: GNS Science
Copyright © 2023 Upstart Press Ltd
GNS Science has asserted its right to be identified as the author of this work.

ISBN: 978-1-77694-002-8

A catalogue record for this book is available at the National Library of New Zealand

Printed by Dongguan P&C Printing Technology Co., Ltd.

10 9 8 7 6 5 4 3 2

Front cover photograph: Thick-shelled bivalves (*Glycymerita*) and gastropods (*Struthiolaria*), from Mead Stream, Marlborough (Miocene, Sw–Tt; 12.98–7.2 Ma).
Back cover photograph: Marlin (Istiophoridae) fish skull, Hampden Beach, Otago (Middle Eocene, Dh; 49.3–45.3 Ma).
Spine photograph: Coral, *Oculina virgosa* (Early Miocene to living, Po–Wq; 21.7–0 Ma).
Title page photograph: Molluscs (e.g. *Guildfordia*, *Magnatica*, *Spissatella*) and brachiopods (e.g. *Pachymagas*) from Otekaike Limestone, South Canterbury (Late Oligocene–Miocene, Lw; 25.2–21.7 Ma).

Contents

How to use this book

- The object of this book is to help you find and identify common New Zealand fossils.
- The first part (Fossils) is a general explanation of fossils and where, how and why they occur. It embraces many kinds of plant and animal fossils found in New Zealand, including microfossils (fossils that are so small that they can only be observed with a microscope).
- The second part (Fossil Preservation) describes aspects of how fossils are preserved, and points out important details to observe for different groups of fossil organisms. Each group of fossils has its own distinctive features – shape, size, texture, colour, type of preservation – which can serve as clues to its identity. This will help you determine what kind of fossil you have found.
- The third part (Geological History of New Zealand) describes the range of fossils known (so far) from New Zealand rocks in terms of the geological timescale: Paleozoic, Mesozoic and Cenozoic. This will help you understand what fossils you can expect to find (and what not to expect) in different parts of New Zealand. The younger Cenozoic rocks are especially widespread in New Zealand, and for this reason Cenozoic fossils are most common and hence dominate this book. For this reason Paleozoic and Mesozoic fossils are limited and no Silurian or Carboniferous fossils are included.
- The fourth part (the photographic guide) presents photographs of the more commonly found macrofossils (fossils that are large enough to be observed easily with the naked eye) of New Zealand, along with essential geological information about their occurrence, distribution and age, and some biological and environmental information about their identity, what they ate and where they lived. *Each photograph is accompanied by a scale bar, the length of which is noted at the end of each fossil description.* Additional interesting facts are included where relevant. This part is colour coded in terms of geological age (periods and epochs),

Fossil hunting can be enjoyed by people of all ages (Magazine Point, Nelson)

so oldest fossils are presented first and youngest last. For each period or epoch, terrestrial fossils are presented first and then the marine fossils. The classification and names of fossils used are based on the 2009 Inventory of New Zealand Biodiversity (Gordon 2009–12). The ages used are based on the 2010 Geological Timescale of New Zealand (Hollis et al. 2010), and the names of geological units (rock groups and formations) are those adopted in the 1:250,000 geological map series.
- This guide is best used with a geological map. It is very easy to use if you know the age of the rock formation from which you have collected your fossils. Location is everything!
- The last part of the guide includes a few common pseudo-fossils, a glossary of terms, further reading and web resources, an index and a detailed geological timescale (after Hollis et al. 2010).

Fossil collecting

Fossil collecting is a fascinating and absorbing activity. Most people can do it. However, you do need good eyesight, a reasonable level of fitness and to be aware of potential environmental hazards while you are collecting. Personal safety is paramount and you should always have a companion. In most instances, fossil extraction requires implements such as a geological hammer and a cold chisel. In soft rocks and sediments, digging implements are appropriate. A hand-lens (magnification ×10) is immensely useful for close examination. Wrapping and storage materials are important, especially for collecting delicate fossils. Knowing where you collected your fossils is very important scientific information. Use maps and GPS. Before you extract any fossils, always make sure you have an accurate and precise record of where the fossil is within the rock or sediment. Take photographs first. The relationship between the fossil and the matrix (rock or sediment) that it is embedded in can be very important information. Some technique is required when using a geological hammer: as a general rule, always strike the rock in a direction that is away from the fossil. This will minimise damage (cracking and breakage) of the fossil. Don't be disheartened if the fossil breaks; it can always be glued back together using standard glues such as PVA.

Fossils

Fossils are very much part of the natural environment. Broadly speaking, fossils are the naturally preserved remains of past life and they are surprisingly common.

The natural environment (air, land, fresh water and sea) is the domain of diverse life (living bacteria, fungi, plants and animals), but it also includes dying and dead organisms. In a perfect world, all organic matter might be preserved forever, but it isn't. Only a tiny fraction becomes fossilised.

Fossils are all about preservation. If it were possible to eliminate the principal agents of destruction, which are oxygen, bacteria,

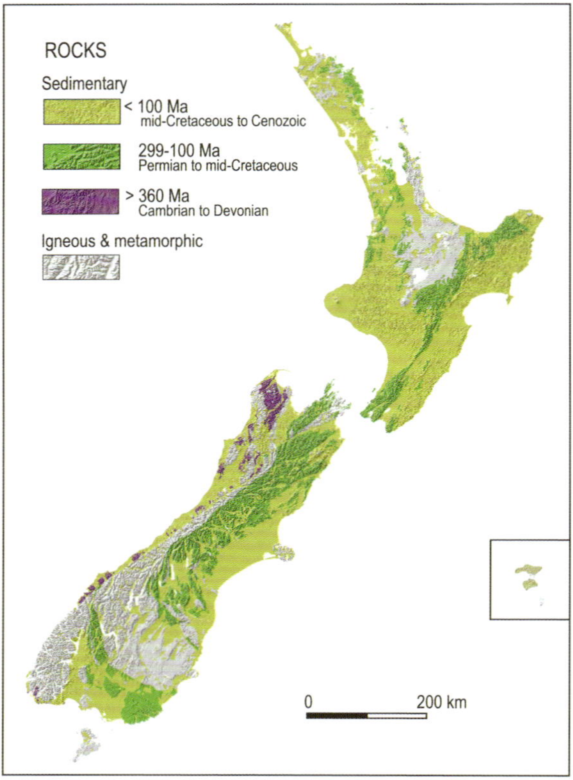

This geological map shows the distribution of major rock types in New Zealand where fossils may be found. Fossils occur in sedimentary rocks and unconsolidated sediments. Rarely are they found in metamorphic and igneous (plutonic and volcanic) rocks

Pliocene fossils, 2.5 million years old, in sedimentary rock (Wilkies Shellbed, Wanganui)

natural radiation (sunlight and cosmic radiation) and mechanical degradation, in theory it would be possible to preserve something forever. There are some places where there is extraordinary preservation such as the Messel Pit (Messel Grube), near Frankfurt in Germany. Here, in oil shales that accumulated in a lake about 48 million years ago in the Eocene Epoch, there are numerous exquisitely preserved fossils (reptiles, fish, birds and mammals) with soft parts preserved (such as skin, hair, internal organs and stomach contents). There is nothing quite like this known from New Zealand – as yet.

Fossils are usually found in sedimentary rocks. All sedimentary rocks start off as sediments such as gravels, sand, silt, mud, peat and soil. The remains of living and dead organisms, especially hard parts such as leaves, twigs, branches, trunks, seeds, nuts, eggshell, shells, carapaces, skeletons, bones, teeth, hair, horns and beaks, can become entrained in sediments that accumulate in soils, swamps, streams, rivers, lakes, estuaries and the seafloor. Sediments, along with organic debris, are naturally moved around by wind, water (including ice), catastrophic events (storms, landslides, earthquakes, tsunami, volcanism and meteorites) and biological agencies (animals, plants and human activity). Organic remains buried in sediments can become preserved and/or mineralised to form fossils. In time, with burial and natural cementation, sediments turn into stone (sedimentary rocks).

There are other less common ways of preserving organic remains in nature, such as desiccation, freezing or entrapment in tree resin. Hence some fossils are found in caves and really dry places, some in frozen places such as in tundra or in ice, and some in amber (fossilised tree resin).

The most conspicuous fossils are shelly fossils of bryozoans, echinoderms, barnacles, brachiopods and molluscs, fossil wood, shark teeth, fossil bone, crab fossils and fossil leaves. But the most common fossils are microscopic, and the most common microfossils are of plankton. These include the mineralised tests or skeletons of single-celled animals (foraminiferans and radiolarians) and single-celled plants (coccoliths and diatoms). Fossil pollen, spores and dinoflagellates (resting cysts or capsules of a group of marine algae) are tough, organic-walled microfossils that occur in vast numbers in marine sediments and sedimentary rocks. Fossil spores and pollen also occur of course in non-marine (terrestrial and freshwater) sediments and sedimentary rocks. Microscopic fossil remains of fungi are also relatively common in terrestrial rocks.

People who study fossils are called paleontologists. Depending on the size or group of fossils being studied, there are macropaleontologists, micropaleontologists, palynologists (who study fossil pollen, spores and dinoflagellates), vertebrate paleontologists and molecular paleontologists (who study fossil molecules including DNA).

There is one special group of 'fossils' that are not the organic remains of living or dead organisms. These are trace fossils (ichnofossils). They include marks, traces, tracks, burrows and deposits that relate to animal and plant behaviour, dead or alive. Trace fossils record an animal's moving, exploring, escaping, hiding, breathing, hunting, feeding, excreting, reproducing, growing, playing, fighting, dying, or resting.

Lastly, there are pseudo-fossils. These are natural features that look like fossils but are not remains or traces of organisms; they are inorganic. These are mostly features relating to crystallisation patterns or mineral growths, and weathering and sedimentary structures produced by water and/or wind.

Cretaceous shellbed fossils in a boulder (Mangahouanga Stream, Hawke's Bay)

Classification of fossils

All organisms, including bacteria, fungi, plants and animals, have been classified by biologists in terms of their distinguishing physical characteristics based on composition, construction (design), shape and size. Biological classification is assumed to reflect the evolutionary relationships between organisms, so that organisms that are classified together in a group are believed to be more closely related than organisms that are classified in different groups. The major groups in biological classification are called Kingdoms and these are progressively subdivided into Phylum, Class, Order, Family, Genus and Species. The same broad classification has been applied to fossils, even though in many cases only hard parts (skeletons, shells, bones and teeth) are known.

The scientific names of fossils, as for all living organisms, are always in two parts, rather like our first name and surname. The creation of scientific names is subject to an internationally agreed convention. Firstly, they are always written in Latin. This is because Latin offers short-hand expression; a lot more words are required to say the same thing in English. Secondly, the genus name begins with a capital letter whereas the species name is all lower case; both are always written in italics. So, the giant ammonite (p. 50) is named *Lytoceras taharoaense*. It looks and sounds complicated, but its meaning is simple and clear. *Lytoceras* is a well-known genus of ammonite from Jurassic rocks all over the world, but this particular species is 'from Taharoa' near Kawhia Harbour in New Zealand, where specimens were first collected, and that is what the name means. Some names appear in inverted commas, signifying that it is not considered a valid name as it was not formally published.

Fossil preservation

Fossil preservation is a fantastically chancy thing because, as discussed above, discarded 'hard parts' decay and disintegrate surprisingly quickly in the natural environment. In general, burial is necessary for fossil preservation to occur. Once buried, other processes start to impact on the buried object, chemical processes in particular. Factors that affect chemical processes are temperature, pressure, accessibility to percolating fluids (porosity and permeability) and the chemistry of these fluids.

Temperature is a significant factor in preservation because no known bacteria can reproduce at temperatures below 4°C, though they can exist below this temperature. (This is why thermostats in fridges are normally set between 0°C and 4°C.)

Types of material being preserved
Preservation varies to a large degree on the nature of the material being preserved. Broadly speaking, there are five types of starting material involved in fossil preservation: calcium carbonate, calcium phosphate, silica and organic polymers.

1. Shelly fossils made of calcium carbonate
Shelly fossils are the most commonly found, conspicuous fossils in New Zealand. They include the following fossil groups: molluscs (rostroconchs, gastropods, bivalves, scaphopods, nautiloids and ammonoids), brachiopods, corals, bryozoans, echinoderms, barnacles, worm tubes, foraminifera and coccoliths.

Shelly fossils can change colour and become heavy due to mineralisation. Why does this happen? All shelly fossils are composed of crystalline minerals (mainly calcite and/or aragonite), which are grown by specialised secretory organs in the living animal. In molluscs and brachiopods this organ is the 'mantle'. This is the thin filmy tissue that lies against the interior of the shell (as in oysters or mussels). The individual calcium carbonate crystals form within a very thin organic matrix which behaves rather like the mortar between concrete blocks in a concrete block construction. Following death and burial, and with percolating fluids, the organic matrix decays, creating space that is then occupied by new crystalline minerals. The resulting fossil shell is therefore mineralised, and because minerals are heavier than organic materials, the fossil shell gains weight.

Much of the colour observed in shells is due to organic molecules, whereas calcite and aragonite are usually colourless or white. However, there are other carbonate minerals (dolomite, ankerite and siderite) which are commonly coloured due to the presence of elements other than calcium, such as magnesium and iron. Common colours are pastel shades of cream, yellow, orange, brown and green. The pink colour in the common intertidal New Zealand brachiopod is due to carotene, a pigment only produced by plants. The animal acquires carotene from the algae that it eats and incorporates it into the calcite crystal lattice as the shell grows.

2. Fossils made of calcium phosphate
Conulariids and vertebrates (bones, teeth and scales).

3. Fossils made of silica
There are only three groups of organisms that have skeletons made of silica: sponges, radiolarians and diatoms. However, because quartz and silicate minerals (such as feldspar, mica and clay) are the most common minerals, silica is very common in the natural environment and often is involved in mineralisation of fossils during the preservation process. Hence, fossils can be 'silicified'. This involves partial or complete replacement of the original material (calcium carbonate, calcium phosphate or cellulose) by silica. Petrified wood is fossil wood that has been silicified.

4. Fossils made of carbohydrate polymers
Plants produce tough organic structures that are composed of carbonate polymers such as cutin (leaves), cellulose (wood), lignin (leaves, seeds, fruits and wood) and sporopollenin (dinoflagellates, pollen and spores).

5. Fossils made of protein polymers
Crustaceans and graptolites are composed of protein polymers. Trilobites, ostracods and decapods (crabs, lobsters and shrimps) are mainly made of chitin with varying degrees of calcification. Graptolites are made from a type of collagen.

Triassic fossils in sedimentary rock, (Kiritehere, Waikato)

Shell preservation: moulds, casts, steinkerns
In order to correctly interpret and identify fossil shells, especially of molluscs and brachiopods, some knowledge of what to expect goes a long way. More often than not, especially in older Mesozoic and Paleozoic rocks, the shell (which is usually recrystallised; rarely is the original shell preserved) has been dissolved by fluids and weather-

ing processes that post-date the transformation (cementation and/ or lithification) from sediment to rock. All that is left is a mould. A shell is three-dimensional and occupies space so it will therefore leave an empty space in the rock if the carbonate is dissolved away. Crack such a rock open and what will be preserved is an external mould which faithfully reflects what the exterior or outer surface of the shell looked like, and an internal mould which faithfully reflects what the inside of the shell looked like. And although you may be looking at the one shell, the inside usually looks very different from the outside.

An external mould (left) and its latex cast (Triassic fossil of marine snail Poroa arata*) (1 cm)*

The inside of brachiopods and bivalve molluscs is notoriously tricky to make sense of because of the nature of the shelly structures developed along the hinge-line, about which the two valves articulate or move with respect to each other.

Articulate brachiopods have interlocking shell structures which hold the valves in correct position when they are opened and closed by an array of muscles. Muscles require strong attachment surfaces (platforms, walls and buttresses), and as the shell grows bigger these shelly surfaces change shape and size and become stronger. As a general rule, the larger the surface area of attachment the stronger the muscle, and the bigger the scar or imprint on the shell interior. The resultant internal moulds of brachiopods can therefore look very strange, with complex but subtle bumps, pits and corrugations. They are very different from an external mould!

External moulds of brachiopods can be equally complicated and bewildering, especially those Paleozoic and Mesozoic forms with spines. In external moulds, spines produce holes or pits. In order to determine what the exterior surface of the shell really looked like, a latex cast is necessary. In general, the shell exterior records the incremental (day-by-day, tide-by-tide, month-by-month) growth of the brachiopod, which is not nearly as easily seen on the inside of the shell. The outside is usually ornamented with radial and/or commarginal structures (ribs, costae, lamellae, carinae, ridges, tubercles, knobs, spines and others). Some brachiopods are punctate; that is, they have tiny canals that penetrate the full thickness of the shell and connect the inside of the shell with the outside world. On well-preserved moulds, these appear as a micro-ornament of tiny regular pits. Most brachiopods are impunctate, but the Mesozoic spiriferinids and Mesozoic to recent terebratulids and terebratellids are punctate.

Bivalve molluscs have very different hinge structures from bra-chiopods, but they serve the same function of ensuring that the shells open and shut correctly. Bivalves have dentition ('teeth') and ligaments along their hinge areas. As with brachiopods, strange holes, slots, bumps, pits, ridges and troughs can be present on internal moulds of bivalves. Muscles keep bivalve shells shut; they effectively work against the ligaments which are 'sprung'. So, when the muscles relax, the shell opens automatically. The inside of a bivalve is normally smooth except for muscle attachment sites. As we well know, the outside can be very ornate indeed and, as with brachiopods, there is a much better record of incremental growth of the shell through time.

Sometimes an internal mould of a closed shell (either brachiopod or bivalve) is found. This is nut-like and is commonly referred to as a steinkern. They can be very revealing because the two valves of both brachiopods and bivalves differ.

In brachiopods the ventral or pedicle valve supports the pedicle (and pedicle foramen or aperture) whereas the dorsal or brachial valve supports the loop (carbonate ribbon or brachia; lophophore support structure; the organism both feeds and respires through the lophophore). They are nevertheless bisymmetrical, being identical if cut in two down the middle at right angles to the commissure (shell margin). Bivalves are different; they are not bisymmetrical. The two valves generally (but not always) look the same from the outside, but this is not true for the inside! The right valve (on your right-hand side when oriented with the anterior away from you and posterior towards you) will have different dentition from the left valve. (This applies in those bivalves with hinge teeth; most do but not all; some are 'edentulous' or lacking teeth.) The hinge structures of the two valves complement each other: a tooth on the right valve will occupy a socket on the left valve and so on.

Geological history of New Zealand

The geological history of New Zealand can be described in terms of three successive episodes during the past 520 million years: Gond-wanaland, Zealandia and New Zealand. Our Gondwanaland history lasted for almost 400 million years and involved plate collision and subduction of the Pacific Plate beneath eastern Gondwana-land. This ended in mid-Cretaceous time about 125 Ma (million years ago) with a dramatic switch to extension tectonics involving rifting of the crust. This caused a large continental fragment of eastern Gondwanaland to break away and become progressively separated as the Tasman Sea floor grew. This small continent, half the size of Australia, is Zealandia. The age of the oldest seafloor in the Tasman Sea tells us that deep ocean has separated Zealandia from Gondwanaland since about 85 Ma. Initially, Zealandia had a substantial land area, but with increasing stretching and crustal thinning, it slowly sank. The land area slowly diminished over the 60 million years from 85 to 25 Ma. At 25 Ma, in Late Oligocene time, most of Zealandia was under the sea. Then there was another tectonic switch. From about 25 Ma, there was a resumption of subduction-related collision or compressional tectonism. This has pushed New Zealand up, giving rise to our mountains and extensive land area; this uplift is ongoing. So, our Zealandian history lasted about 100 million years, and our New Zealand history relates to the last 25 million years. Today, New Zealand may be thought of as the emergent part (less than 7 per cent) of the otherwise sunken continent of Zealandia. The fossil record preserved in New Zealand rocks faithfully reflects this remarkable history.

New Zealand's fossil record

This is an account of what kinds of fossils we have in New Zealand in terms of geological time and the three major episodes in our history: Gondwanaland, Zealandia and New Zealand. This will help you determine what fossils you can expect to find and where. According to the 2009 New Zealand Inventory of Biodiversity, 14,700 named fossils are known from New Zealand. This compares with about 56,250 named living organisms (terrestrial and marine) in the country today.

GONDWANALAND from 520 to 125 Ma; Cambrian to Cretaceous

Paleozoic Era This era includes the Cambrian, Ordovician, Silurian, Devonian, Carboniferous and Permian Periods of geological time, spanning some 290 million years from 542 to 252 million years ago.

- **Cambrian Period** (542–488 Ma): The oldest fossils in New Zealand are of Middle Cambrian age, about 510 million years old. Only Middle and Late Cambrian fossils are known from New Zealand rocks. They are indicative of sea life living at the time and include sponges, brachiopods, molluscs, trilobites and conodonts (dental apparatus of primitive fish). Cambrian fossils are known from Cobb Valley (in North-west Nelson) and Springs Junction (in West Nelson).
- **Ordovician Period** (488–444 Ma): New Zealand Ordovician fossils include corals, brachiopods, trilobites, crustaceans, conodonts and abundant graptolites. However, many groups of organisms are absent and no significant bryozoans or vertebrates are known. New Zealand has a particularly good record of Ordovician time in terms of graptolites, one of the most complete known anywhere. The best Ordovician sequences are in North-west Nelson at Aorangi Mine, Cobb Valley, Mt Patriarch, Takaka Valley and Wangapeka Valley. Other localities are in the Baton River (West Nelson) and at Cape Providence and Preservation Inlet (Fiordland).

- **Silurian Period** (444–416 Ma): This was a time of major expansion for many of the shelly marine invertebrate groups that had first appeared in Cambrian and Ordovician times. However, Silurian time is poorly represented in New Zealand. Silurian fossils are known from just two localities in North-west Nelson (Pikikiruna Range and Wangapeka Valley). Known fossils include six species of brachiopod of Middle Silurian age. A few coral, crinoid and bivalve fossils are also known.
- **Devonian Period** (416–359 Ma): During Devonian time, often called the 'Age of Fishes', sharks and spiny fish first appeared as did large fish, some covered with massive armoured plates or thick scales. There is no record of land fossils in the New Zealand Devonian. However, there is a good record of sea life, including bivalves, brachiopods, trilobites, corals, stomatoporoids (sponges), bryozoans, crinoids, echinoderms, conodonts and tentaculites (small, conical, tube-like fossils, possibly related to bryozoans). Devonian fossils are known from three areas: near Reefton, Baton River (110 km north of Reefton), and near Lake Haupiri (North Westland).
- **Carboniferous Period** (359–299 Ma): Carboniferous time is virtually unrepresented in New Zealand. Only one certain fossil locality has been described: Kakahu, South Canterbury. The only fossils from Kakahu are conodonts and fragments of fish scales, and it is generally thought that the rocks (marble and chert) that these fossils come from are large blocks of displaced rock within much younger rocks.
- **Permian Period** (299–251 Ma): Permian time is moderately well-represented in New Zealand. Permian fossils are known from only a few localities in the North Island and are the oldest fossils known from there. Middle Permian fusuline foraminifera and other shelly fossils (bryozoans, brachiopods and molluscs) occur in limestone in Whangaroa Bay and Moturoa Island (Bay of Islands) in Northland, and Middle Permian radiolarians and conodonts occur in Red Rocks near Wellington. Permian rocks are more extensive and widespread in the South Island, especially in the Nelson region and Southland (e.g. near Clinton), but also in a few localities in North Otago and Mid Canterbury. The oldest Permian fossils in New Zealand are from the Skippers Range and Takitimu Mountains and the richest fossil localities are in the Wairaki Hills north of Ohai (Southland). Permian fossils are dominated by brachiopods, bivalves, gastropods and bryozoans. Less common are scaphopods, rostroconchs (molluscs), conulariids, echinoderms and trilobites. Almost no cephalopods have been collected. Distinctive mussel-like bivalves with characteristic prismatic shell structure (Atomodesmatinae) are the most common Permian fossils in New Zealand. They were locally so abundant that the disintegrated remains of these shells accumulated in vast sheets to form limestone; unusual because the limestone is mostly redeposited, almost devoid of any other fossils, and lacking any significant mineral sand component. Rare vertebrate fossils include conodonts and fish scales. The oldest

The genus Monotis (Entomonotis) *of bivalves are common Late Triassic fossils from New Zealand (1 cm)*

plant fossils known from New Zealand are of Late Permian age and are found in rocks north of Ohai and also near Clinton in Southland. They include leaf fossils, spores, pollen and wood. About 10 specimens of *Glossopteris* leaf have been found, but no actual terrestrial rocks are known from New Zealand in this period. Spectacular trace fossils are known from some localities, most notably at Mokomoko Inlet near Bluff.

Mesozoic Era The end of Permian time, 251 million years ago, was punctuated by the most profound extinction event recognised within the last 500 million years. It brought the Paleozoic Era to a natural close and ushered in the Mesozoic Era. The nature of this event is uncertain but one interpretation is comet collision. Rock formations that span the Permian–Triassic boundary are recognised in New Zealand, but precise fossil and age determination have not yet been established. The Mesozoic Era includes the Triassic, Jurassic and Cretaceous Periods and spanned 186 million years, between 251 and 65 million years ago.

- **Triassic Period** (251–200 Ma): Triassic time is noted for the global rise to dominance of marine molluscs and marine reptiles, while on land the earliest dinosaurs and mammals appeared. However, no Triassic dinosaur or mammal fossils are known from New Zealand. Triassic time is particularly well-represented in New Zealand by widespread marine sedimentary rocks. Fossils include: radiolarians, foraminifera, hydrozoans, conulariids, bryozoans, echinoderms (especially crinoids), brachiopods and molluscs (scaphopods, gastropods, bivalves, nautiloids and ammonoids), ostracods and other crustaceans. Vertebrate fossils of conodonts, fish and marine reptiles are present, but they are generally rare. Dinoflagellates first appear in Late Triassic rocks. No terrestrial animal fossils are known except for a labyrinthodont amphibian. Plant fossils (wood and leaves including *Dicroidium*) and fossil seeds, spores and pollen are also present in places throughout Triassic rocks, notably in the Canterbury 'greywackes'. These fossil plants are representative of Triassic Gondwanaland vegetation. Fossiliferous Triassic rock sequences are scattered throughout both North and South Islands, but are richest in Nelson (Barnicoat Range), Southland (Kaihiku, Hokonui and Taringatura Ranges and Wairaki Hills) and the King Country coast south-west of Auckland, between Awakino and Albatross Point. The oldest easily accessible fossils in the North Island are exposed on the coast to the immediate south of Kiritehere (near Marokopa). Much of the greywacke rock of New Zealand is of Triassic age.

- **Jurassic Period** (200–145 Ma): Jurassic time is noted for the decline of brachiopods and the rise of the ammonites (a particular group of ammonoids), and another group of squid-like cephalopods, the belemnites. On land, the dinosaurs and birds rose to prominence, and flowering plants began to appear. In New Zealand, marine fossils were fully representative of the seas of the time and include dinoflagellates, calcispheres, radiolarians, foraminifera, bryozoans, corals, echinoderms (especially crinoids), brachiopods and molluscs (scaphopods, gastropods, bivalves, nautiloids, ammonites and belemnites), ostracods and other crustaceans, and rare sharks and bony fish. A single dinosaur fossil (theropod hand bone) is known from near Port Waikato, North Island. Terrestrial sequences are known in several localities with especially well-preserved tree stumps *in situ*, along with associated plant beds. Fossil wood, leaves, seeds, spores and pollen have been documented from many places. The oldest fossil insect (a proto-weta) recorded from New Zealand is Jurassic. Fossil-bearing Jurassic rocks occur in both North and South Islands, but they are especially rich in the Awakino to Kawhia region of the North Island, and the Catlins area of Southland. The largest known fossils in New Zealand are probably the fossil logs preserved at Curio Bay, Southland. These are of Middle Jurassic age.

- **Cretaceous Period** (145–65.5 Ma): Cretaceous time is noted for the global rise to dominance of calcareous plankton including coccoliths or nannofossils (chalk-forming single-celled algae) and calcareous foraminifera (single-celled animals) as well as marine reptiles (mosasaurs), and on land the radiation of the flowering plants (angiosperms). The oldest New Zealand Cretaceous fossils are fossil plankton: dinoflagellates, nannofossils, radiolarians and foraminiferans, of earliest Cretaceous age. A relatively long period of Early Cretaceous time is largely unrepresented by fossils in New Zealand. This 'absence' represents the end of our Gondwanaland history and the onset of our Zealandian history at about 125 Ma.

Cape Farewell, north-western South Island, features Cretaceous–Paleocene coal measures overlain by Late Oligocene marine sandstones, mudstones and limestones

ZEALANDIA from 125 to 25 Ma; Cretaceous to Oligocene

Mid- to Late Cretaceous marine fossils include dinoflagellates, nannofossils, radiolarians, foraminiferans, bryozoans, corals, ostracods, molluscs (scaphopods, gastropods, bivalves and in particular the inoceramids, ammonites and belemnites), brachiopods, echinoderms, crustaceans and vertebrates (fish and marine reptiles). Terrestrial sequences include coals and associated sediments with wood, leaf, seed and palynomorph fossils. The oldest fossil flowers known from New Zealand are of Late Cretaceous age. Rare insect and vertebrate fossils are known. A single locality in a tributary of the Te Hoe River (inland Hawke's Bay, North Island) has produced fragmentary dinosaur, turtle, pterosaur and perhaps bird fossils from within shallow marine sediments of Late Cretaceous age. During much of Cretaceous time, New Zealand was situated within the polar circle.

When Zealandia rifted away from Gondwanaland during mid- to Late Cretaceous time, it carried a 'cargo' of plants and animals that were derived from Gondwanaland species. With isolation and time, they evolved into forms unique to Zealandia. It is presumed that this cargo included the ancestors of many of New Zealand's modern plants and animals. However, the fossil record for most native species (except trees and ferns) of modern New Zealand is so poor that no certain or direct evidence can be or has been established. Mammals, including marsupials, may well have been present. There is a possible record of a small Miocene mammal from Central Otago.

Cenozoic Era

The end of the Mesozoic Era and onset of the Cenozoic Era is dramatically marked by the Cretaceous–Cenozoic (or Tertiary) extinction event caused by a meteorite impact 65.5 Ma that struck

A black band of rock at Ward Beach, Marlborough preserves the Cretaceous–Paleogene boundary

Earth in present-day Mexico. The effects of this collision were profound and caused widespread destruction of the base of the food chain, both on land and in the sea, with consequent extinction of many higher organisms. All species greater than 25 kg in size were wiped out. This included all dinosaurs except the birds. In aquatic environments, many single-celled planktonic plants and all marine reptiles, ammonites and belemnites became extinct. With the slow return to normality on Earth, mammals and birds rose to dominance. Rock formations that preserve a record of this event occur in several places in New Zealand, but most notably in Marlborough and at Te Kaukau Point (the south-eastern tip of the North Island). The Cenozoic Era is subdivided into three periods: Paleogene, Neogene and Quaternary.

Paleogene Period: Paleocene, Eocene and Oligocene Epochs.

- **Paleocene Epoch** (65.5–55.8 Ma): This was a time of rapid re-establishment of life on Earth. Much of Zealandia was still above sea level, but it was slowly sinking in response to rifting. Zealandia had moved well north of the polar circle. Relatively cool-water marine fossils are preserved. Shallow-water marine Paleocene fossils are not as common or as diverse as deeper water assemblages. Fossils include dinoflagellates, radiolarians, nannofossils, foraminiferans, bryozoans, brachiopods, molluscs (gastropods, bivalves and nautiloids) and vertebrates. New Zealand has some of the oldest known penguinoid and other marine bird fossils. Terrestrial coal accumulation persisted through the Paleocene with associated wood, leaf, spore and pollen fossils.
- **Eocene Epoch** (55.8–33.9 Ma): This was a long period of expansion for mammals along with the evolution of higher plants and in particular diversification of the grasses. New Zealand is well endowed with fossiliferous Eocene sediments that record a continued foundering of Zealandia and consequent reduction of

land mass area. Conditions were warmer, as indicated by a variety of climatic indicators. Fossils include: dinoflagellates, diatoms, radiolarians, foraminiferans, bryozoans, corals, echinoderms, brachiopods; scaphopod, gastropod, bivalve and nautiloid molluscans; ostracod, cirripede and decapod crustaceans; and some vertebrates – cetaceans mainly, but also sharks, bony fish, turtles and marine birds. The oldest cetacean fossils in New Zealand are of late Middle Eocene age. Terrestrial coal accumulation continued through Eocene time with attendant wood, leaf, seed and palynomorph fossils in associated sediments. At times in the Eocene conditions were warm enough for mangroves and in particular warm-water molluscs. It is generally understood that the ultimate origin of most of New Zealand's oil and gas reserves (mainly in offshore and onshore Taranaki) is coal of latest Cretaceous to Eocene age. Eocene limestone is composed largely of the fossil skeletal remains of bryozoans, echinoderms and foraminifera, but it was restricted to warm, shallow reaches of Zealandia, such as are preserved in the Chatham Islands. Eocene sediments are widespread throughout New Zealand.

- **Oligocene Epoch** (33.9–23.03 Ma): During this time Antarctica became isolated, with establishment of the Circum-Antarctic Current, and southern polar ice sheets formed. These events had a profound effect on all life in the southern hemisphere, including Zealandia. During Late Oligocene time, foundering of Zealandia reached its zenith with maximum flooding by the sea. Very little land area remained. This has given rise to the concept of the 'Oligocene bottleneck' in New Zealand: the loss of terrestrial habitat and a supposed restriction in biodiversity. Shallow-water limestone sediment accumulation was widespread. The fossil record is rich and diverse, but it is dominated by invertebrates with calcite shells or skeletons that preserve well in limestone: foraminiferans, bryozoans, corals, brachiopods, echinoderms, molluscs with calcite shells, ostracod and cirripede crustaceans, and vertebrates such as bony fish, sharks, cetaceans and penguins.

The Waipara River area, North Canterbury, features Eocene mudstones (left of river) and Oligocene limestone cliffs

In New Zealand there are no recorded Oligocene sea turtle fossils which are known from Eocene and Miocene sediments. Deeper marine sediments are known, with radiolarian and diatom fossils. Terrestrial fossils are less common than in the Eocene, but they include wood, leaf, seed and palynomorph fossils. No terrestrial animal fossils are known. Oligocene sediments are widespread throughout New Zealand.

NEW ZEALAND from 25 to 0 Ma; Oligocene to present day

Neogene Period: Miocene and Pliocene Epochs.

● **Miocene Epoch** (23.03–5.33 Ma): This epoch is characterised by the appearance and continued development of animals and plants ancestral to modern forms. In New Zealand, the modern plate boundary configuration involving vigorous collision between the Pacific and Australian Plates commenced, uplifting a wide part of the plate boundary zone within Zealandia to form New Zealand. With the emergence of land, swamps

Ototoka Beach, Wanganui, features Nukumaruan (Neogene) sandstones and mudstones overlain by shell conglomerate

A Pleistocene fossil of Nothofagus *cf.* cliffortioides, *one of the 'southern beech' species (1 cm)*

became established in parts of New Zealand with a subdued topography (Southland, Waikato and King Country) leading to widespread Miocene lignite accumulation. Elsewhere within the New Zealand land mass, mountain building had commenced. Diverse Miocene sediments are widespread throughout New Zealand. Marine fossils include: dinoflagellates, diatoms, radiolarians, foraminiferans, bryozoans, corals, echinoderms, brachiopods, molluscs (scaphopods, gastropods, bivalves and nautiloids), crustaceans (ostracods, cirripedes and decapods) and vertebrates (bony fish, sharks, turtles, cetaceans, penguins and seals). Terrestrial plant fossils include wood, leaves, flowers, fruits, seeds, coconuts, pollen and spores. Other terrestrial fossils include insects, crustaceans, crocodiles, turtles, reptiles (including tuatara), birds (including ratites), freshwater fish, bats and possibly other small mammals mentioned previously. Several richly fossiliferous lake deposits are known from Central Otago and Southland. Warmer conditions prevailed at times during the Miocene in New Zealand.

- **Pliocene Epoch** (5.33–2.59 Ma): This epoch saw the advent of our immediate human ancestors with the appearance of the hominid primates in Africa. In New Zealand, Pliocene environmental conditions and life were similar to those of the Miocene. Pliocene sediments are widespread throughout New Zealand, but they are not nearly as voluminous or as fossiliferous as the Miocene record. The richest marine macrofossil localities are located in Hawke's Bay and the Wanganui region. The Wanganui Basin is well known for its foraminifera-rich and mollusc-rich Pliocene marine successions, and shellbeds are also common on the east coast of the North Island. New Zealand Pliocene marine fossils include dinoflagellates, diatoms, radiolarians, foraminiferans, bryozoans, corals, echinoderms, brachiopods, molluscs (scaphopods, gastropods, bivalves and nautiloids), crustaceans (ostracods, cirripedes and decapods) and vertebrates (fish, sharks, cetaceans, marine birds and seals). Terrestrial fossils are not common but include wood, leaves, seeds, pollen and spores; freshwater molluscs, fish and very rare terrestrial birds are also known.

The gastropod fossil Pelicaria zelandiae *is representative of the Mid-Pliocene (1 cm)*

Quaternary Period: Pleistocene, Holocene and Anthropocene Epochs.

- **Pleistocene Epoch** (2.59 Ma–13,000 years ago): This is best known globally for 'the ice ages'. New Zealand has one of the finest Pleistocene fossil records known globally, especially in the Wanganui area of the North Island. Marine fossils include nannofossils, foraminiferans, bryozoans, brachiopods, molluscs (scaphopods, gastropods and bivalves), echinoderms, crustaceans (ostracods, cirripedes and decapods) and vertebrates (fish, shark teeth, cetaceans, penguins and seals). New Zealand Pleistocene terrestrial fossils include diatoms, molluscs (bivalves and gastropods), insects, fish and plant fossils (wood, leaves, seeds, spores and pollen). The oldest known fossils of a few of New Zealand's iconic native birds (such as kiwi) and animals are of Pleistocene age, and have been collected primarily from peat swamp and cave

A rare find: a spectacular fossil fish in sandstone of Early Eocene age with exceptional preservation of scales and bones. Collected on Pitt Island (Chatham Islands)

deposits. Pleistocene sediments are widespread throughout New Zealand. The coldest phase of the last glaciation (ice age), was approximately 20,000 years ago, and at this time sea level was about 125 m below present and average surface temperatures were about 5°C below present, so Auckland would have had temperatures similar to those that Invercargill has today. With sea level so low, the surface area of the New Zealand land mass was considerably greater than it is now. There were land connections between the North, South and Stewart Islands, as well as many of the smaller present-day offshore islands.

- **Holocene Epoch** (13,000–AD 1400): The Holocene was a time of slow global warming. Modern sea level attained its present height about 6000 years ago and has remained very stable until the latter part of last century. In New Zealand, Holocene fossils are the same as for the Pleistocene, but they are generally not mineralised. The oldest known fossils of many well-known native birds and terrestrial animals are no older than Holocene. The oldest evidence of human, dog and rat remains and/or presence in New Zealand post-dates the relatively widespread (from Bay of Plenty to Bay of Islands) volcanic ash deposited by the Kaharoa Eruption of Mount Tarawera dated at AD 1314 +/– 12 years. There is no recognised oral record or tradition of the Kaharoa Eruption within Maori iwi. This geological reasoning implies the organised arrival of ancestral Maori in the upper North Island sometime in the early 1300s but after the Kaharoa Eruption.

- **Anthropocene Epoch** (AD 1400–present day): The Anthropocene Epoch relates to the dramatic impact of humanity upon the Earth's surface. As yet informal in terms of definition, the onset of the Anthropocene probably relates to the 'agricultural revolution' which began more than 600 years ago in the early fifteenth century.

Paleontologists collecting fossils at New Zealand's first documented fossil locality (collected by Dieffenbach in 1839 but described by Gray in 1842) at Tioriori, northern coast of Chatham Island. The fossils are oysters of Early Eocene age.

Dorypyge sp.

Phylum Arthropoda **Class** Trilobita **Family** Dorypigidae **Age** Middle Cambrian Xfl–Xun (506–503 Ma) **Rock units** Haupiri Group (Tasman Formation), Takaka Terrane, Cobb Valley (NW Nelson) **Description** Medium-sized with a large pygidium, a spinose thorax with 7–10 segments, and an elongate glabella often with concave sides; distinctive spines **Original shell** Calcite **Habitat** Marine, found in shallow water limestone to deep-sea shale **Diet** Diverse; small plants and animals **Notes** Trilobites were immensely successful, existing for 250 million years (Early Cambrian to Late Permian); most had excellent eyesight, with calcite crystal lenses. (5 mm)

Nepea sp.

Phylum Arthropoda **Class** Trilobita **Family** Nepeidae **Age** Middle Cambrian Xfl–Xun (506–503 Ma) **Rock units** Haupiri Group (Tasman Formation), Takaka Terrane, Cobb Valley (NW Nelson) **Description** This specimen has very large eyes and wonderfully

crumpled glabellar tubercle and boss **Original shell** Calcite **Habitat** Marine, found in shallow water limestone to deep-sea shale **Diet** Diverse; small plants and animals **Notes** There are very few places in New Zealand where you can easily find trilobites; mostly in Abel Tasman National Park; Trilobite Rock, Cobb Valley; they are cryptic fossils, occurring as fragments in thin layers of shell-hash within grey limestone; first discovered in New Zealand by a Nelson schoolboy (Martin Simpson) in 1948. (5 mm)

Didymograptus (Corymbograptus) v-flexus

(*See* **a** in photo below) **Phylum** Hemichordata **Class** Graptolithina **Family** Dichograptidae **Age** Middle Ordovician Vca (471.0–470.0 Ma) **Rock units** Golden Bay Group (Aorangi Mine Formation), Buller Terrane, SW of Collingwood (NW Nelson) **Description** This form has two pendent, horizontal or reclined elongate stipes that look like saw blades; 20–600 mm in length **Original structure** Organic collagen compound **Habitat** Marine, pelagic; they floated at various water depths **Diet** Filter-feeding on plankton and organic particles **Notes** Graptolites preserve as silvery-grey casts of flattened rhabdosomes; the rhabdosome is comprised of symmetrical stipes made up of rows of cup-like thecae; graptolites existed for 125 million years (Middle Cambrian to Middle Devonian). (1 cm)

Goniograptus macer

(*See* **b** in photo below) **Phylum** Hemichordata **Class** Graptolithina **Family** Sigmagraptidae **Age** Middle Ordovician Vca (471.0–470.0 Ma) **Rock units** Golden Bay Group (Aorangi Mine Formation), Buller Terrane, SW of Collingwood (NW Nelson) **Description** This form shows remarkable symmetry based upon four diverging zigzag main stipes which split off alternate branches, creating an open, bush-like colony; 30–300 mm in length **Original structure** Organic collagen compound **Habitat** Marine, pelagic; they floated at various water depths **Diet** Filter-feeding on plankton and organic particles **Notes** This form is distinctive because of its divaricating morphology and thin, stick-like stipes. (1 cm)

Graptolites Didymograptus (Corymbograptus) v-flexus (*a*) *and* Goniograptus macer (*b*)

Isograptus victoriae maximodivergens

(*See* **a** in photo below) **Phylum** Hemichordata **Class** Graptolithina **Family** Isograptidae **Age** Middle Ordovician Vca (471.0–470.0 Ma) **Rock units** Golden Bay Group (Aorangi Mine Formation), Buller Terrane, SW of Collingwood (NW Nelson) **Description** The *Isograptus* rhabdosome has two reclined, robust stipes; this form is large and broad and has an open V shape; 4–40 mm in length **Original structure** Organic collagen compound **Habitat** Marine and pelagic; they floated at various water depths **Diet** Filter-feeding on plankton and organic particles **Notes** This broad-bladed form resembles the wings of a sycamore seed. (1 cm)

Isograptus caduceus australis

(*See* **b** in photo below) **Phylum** Hemichordata **Class** Graptolithina **Family** Isograptidae **Age** Middle Ordovician Vca (471.0–470.0 Ma) **Rock units** Golden Bay Group (Aorangi Mine Formation), Buller Terrane, SW of Collingwood (NW Nelson) **Description** This form of *Isograptus* has a narrower V shape and narrower stipes than *Isograptus victoriae maximodivergens* (see above entry); note juvenile individual in photo; 4–40 mm in length **Original structure** Organic collagen compound **Habitat** Marine and pelagic; they floated at various water depths **Diet** Filter-feeding on plankton and organic particles **Notes** Graptolites were pelagic and cosmopolitan, living in all seas; as fossils they are most conspicuous in fine-grained sedimentary rocks such as black shales and slates. (1 cm)

Graptolites Isograptus victoriae maximodivergens *(**a**) and* Isograptus caduceus australis *(**b**)*

Phylum Cnidaria **Class** Anthozoa **Subclass** Rugosa **Family** Eridophyllidae **Age** Early Devonian Jem (407.0–397.5 Ma) **Rock units** Reefton Group (Reefton) **Description** Solitary or colonial, reef-forming corals with regular-spaced, long, alternate radial septae as is evident in the visible calice of the corallum, with a well-defined theca **Original shell** Aragonite **Habitat** Shallow warm water **Diet** Filter-feeding on plankton and suspended organic matter; may or may not have supported symbiotic algae **Notes** At least eight different corals have been recorded from Devonian formations in New Zealand; this diversity indicates prevailing warm seas. (1 cm)

Chonetes sp.

Internal mould of ventral valve

Phylum Brachiopoda **Class** Articulata **Family** Chonetidae **Age** Early Devonian Jem (407.0–397.5 Ma) **Rock units** Reefton Group (Reefton) **Description** *Chonetes* has spines projecting from the hinge-line, but not from the rest of the shell exterior; small to medium-sized shells; distinctive semicircular outline; radial ornament of regularly spaced and sized, narrow, rounded costellae **Original shell** Calcite **Habitat** Free-living on a silt, sand or limestone substrate **Diet** Filter-feeding on plankton and suspended organic matter **Notes** Relatively common in siltstone. (5 mm)

Euryspirifer coxi

Internal mould of ventral valve

Phylum Brachiopoda **Class** Articulata **Family** Spiriferidae **Age** Early Devonian Jem (407.0–397.5) Ma **Rock units** Reefton Group (Reefton) **Description** Medium to large biconvex impunctate transverse brachiopods with spiralia (looped internal skeletal ribbons of calcite), an extended elongate hinge and wing-like appearance with radial folds. **Original shell** Calcite **Habitat** Attached to substrate by a pedicle; lying on soft sandy and silty seafloors **Diet** Filter-feeding on plankton and suspended organic matter **Notes** Elegant and distinctive; shellbed forming; best preserved in siltstone or mudstone; the extended hinge line may have served to stabilise the shell on the seafloor. (1 cm)

Mauispirifer hectori

Internal moulds of two ventral valves

Phylum Brachiopoda **Class** Articulata **Family** Spiriferidae **Age** Early Devonian Jem (407.0–397.5 Ma) **Rock units** Reefton Group (Reefton) **Description** Small to medium-sized shells with strong radial plicae and a prominent sulcus **Original shell** Calcite **Habitat** Attached to substrate (sediment particle, rock) by a pedicle; living on soft or hard substrates **Diet** Filter-feeding on plankton and suspended organic matter **Notes** A very attractive brachiopod that is easily distinguished from the much more elongate *Euryspirifer* by its small size and more equant shape. (1 cm)

Lyriopecten casterorum

Internal mould of left valve with external of right valve superimposed

Phylum Mollusca **Class** Bivalvia **Family** Pterinopectinidae **Age** Early Devonian Jem (407.0–397.5 Ma) **Rock units** Reefton Group (Reefton) **Description** Small to large, thin-shelled with clearly defined auricles; shells orbicular to subrhomboidal; strong intercalating radial ribs and finer, close-spaced, commarginal growth lines **Original shell** Calcite and aragonite **Habitat** Epifaunal; attached to substrate by a short byssus **Diet** Filter-feeding on plankton and suspended organic matter **Notes** Best preserved in mudstone; occurs with another pectinoid (*Pterinopecten*) which has very regular, fine radial ribs of equal strength. (5 mm)

Paleodora reeftonensis

Phylum Mollusca **Class** Bivalvia **Family** Sinodoridae **Age** Early Devonian Jem (407.0–397.5 Ma) **Rock units** Reefton Group (Reefton) **Description** Small to large, elongate, inequivalve, thin shells with prominent commarginal ridges on the anterior; the right valve is slightly convex whereas the left valve is very flat **Original shell** Calcite **Habitat** Infaunal burrower **Diet** Probably a deposit-feeder, extracting organic particles and plankton from sediment **Notes** Normally found in mudstone; comparable to modern *Myodora* in shape, size and habitat; *Paleodora* is relatively common and occurs with a diversity of other infaunal molluscs. (5 mm)

External mould

Glossopteris ampla

Kingdom Plantae **Order** Glossopteridales **Age** Permian YAr–YAf (273.0–260.4 Ma) **Rock units** Productus Creek Group (Southland) **Description** A broad leaf; about 150 mm long and 65 mm

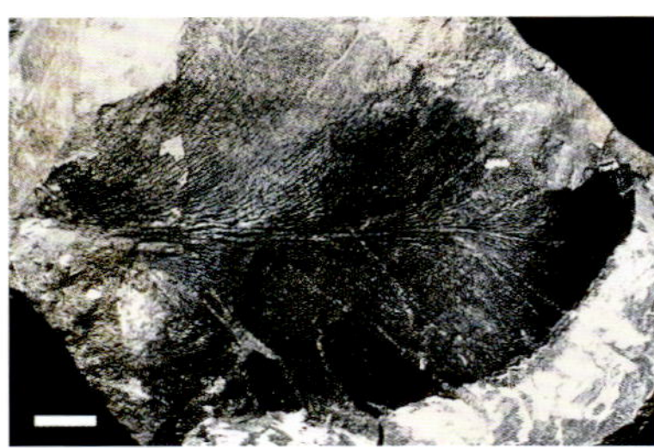

wide; rounded or emarginate apex; smooth margin; midvein wide and narrows towards apex; close secondary veins depart midvein at an acute angle but curve outwards **Notes** Oldest named fossil plant known from New

Zealand; other Permian plant fossils occur in the Maitai Group near Pukerau (Southland) and Rai Valley (Marlborough); could occur in the Torlesse Supergroup of South Canterbury; provides significant evidence that New Zealand was part of Gondwanaland. (1 cm)

Terrakea brachythaerum

Phylum Brachiopoda **Superfamily** Productacea **Family** Monticuliferidae **Age** Middle Permian YAr (273.0–266.5 Ma) **Rock units** Productus Creek Group (Southland) **Description** Small to

medium-sized, thick shells; elongate, cuplike, convex ventral valve; slightly concave dorsal valve; short, stubby spines hug the shell surface; weak commarginal wrinkles and fine radial ornament; large muscle scars **Original shell** Calcite **Habitat** Reclining within or on silt; supported by hollow spines **Diet**

Internal mould of ventral valve

Filter-feeding on plankton and suspended organic matter **Notes** Relatively common, shellbed-forming in places; at least 30 forms of productid brachiopod are recognised in New Zealand Permian rocks. (5 mm)

Capillonia brevisulcus

Internal mould of ventral valve

Phylum Brachiopoda **Family** Rugosochonetidae **Age** Late Permian YDp–YDm (260.4–250.4 Ma) **Rock units** Maitai Group (Nelson, Southland), Productus Creek Group (Southland) **Description** Transverse to rectangular, small to medium-sized shells; smooth, convex ventral valve and a finely capillate, concave dorsal valve, with distinctive spines on hinge-line **Original shell** Calcite **Habitat** Reclining within or on silt, supported by spines **Diet** Filter-feeding on plankton and suspended organic matter **Notes** Relatively common in some formations; best preserved in siltstone. (5 mm)

Tomiopsis parallela

Phylum Brachiopoda **Family** Ingelarellidae **Age** Middle to Late Permian YDp (266.5–253.8 Ma) **Rock units** Maitai Group (Nelson, Southland) **Description** Medium-sized, biconvex, elliptical shells; impunctate, thick-shelled; short hinge; incurved umbones; lacking prominent radial ribs, but with a weak sulcus on the pedicle valve; smooth but with distinctive micro-ornament of tiny pits arranged concentrically; interior with elongate median crura **Original shell** Calcite **Habitat** Attached by a pedicle **Diet** Filter-feeding on plankton and suspended organic matter **Notes** Relatively common spiriferid group in New Zealand Permian formations (over 20 species); very useful for determining relative age succession. (1 cm)

Internal mould of ventral valve

Aperispirifer lethamensis

Ventral valve

Phylum Brachiopoda **Class** Articulata **Family** Trigonotretidae **Age** Early to Middle Permian YAr (273.0–266.5 Ma) **Rock units** Productus Creek Group (Southland) **Description** Medium-sized to large, biconvex, thick-shelled, impunctate shells with long hinge-line, high umbones and numerous close-spaced radial ribs; several prominent commarginal growth stops; pedicle valve with pronounced sulcus **Original shell** Calcite **Habitat** Attached to substrate by a pedicle **Diet** Filter-feeding on plankton and suspended organic matter **Notes** Relatively common spiriferid group in New Zealand Permian formations; well-preserved specimens are very handsome and showy. (1 cm)

Peruvispira imbricata

External mould and latex cast

Phylum Mollusca **Class** Gastropoda **Superfamily** Pleurotomariacea **Family** Phymatopleuridae **Age** Early to Middle Permian YAr–YAf (273.0–260.4 Ma) **Rock units** Maitai Group (Nelson, Southland), Productus Creek Group (Southland) **Description** Small with high spire; slit (siphonal canal) of moderate depth and a subvertical selenizone bounded by two prominent carinae; ornament of fine radial growth lines **Original shell** Aragonite **Habitat** Shallow water **Diet** Uncertain; probably grazing on algae **Notes** This is the most common gastropod in New Zealand Permian rocks (more than six species); they generally occur as external moulds; best preserved in siltstone. (1 cm)

Etheripecten striatura

External mould and latex rubber cast (inset) of left valve

Phylum Mollusca **Class** Bivalvia **Family** Etheripectinidae **Age** Late Permian YDp (260.4–253.8 Ma) **Rock units** Maitai Group, Productus Creek Group (Southland) **Description** Small pectinoid shells, similar to modern fan-shells, with left valve convex and right valve less so, with well-defined auricles, and with ornament of prominent narrow, radial plicae and numerous subordinate radial threads, and commarginal growth lines **Original shell** Calcite and aragonite **Habitat** Attached to the substrate by a byssus **Diet** Filter-feeding on plankton and organic matter suspended in the water **Notes** More than 20 different pectinoids are recorded from New Zealand Permian formations; as with their modern relatives, they are attractive to collect. (1 cm)

Trabeculatia trabecula

Phylum Mollusca **Class** Bivalvia **Family** Inoceramidae **Subfamily** Atomodesmatinae **Age** Late Permian YDp (260.4–253.8 Ma) **Rock units** Maitai Group (Nelson, Southland), Productus Creek Group (Southland) **Description** Medium-sized to large, smooth clams; equivalve; mussel-shaped, moderately globose; distinctive thick hinge; prominent beaks; ornament of gentle corrugations; obvious muscle scars **Original shell** Calcite and aragonite; outer shell of distinctive prismatic calcite (like horse mussels) **Habitat** Attached by a byssus **Diet** Filter-feeding on plankton and suspended organic matter; possibly had symbiotic algae **Notes** Comminuted atomodesmatinid prismatic shell is limestone-forming; the most common fossil in New Zealand Permian formations. (1 cm)

Internal moulds of left valve (right) and right valve (left)

Myonia elongata

Phylum Mollusca **Class** Bivalvia **Family** Edmondiidae **Age** Middle Permian YAf (266.5–260.4 Ma) **Rock units** Productus Creek Group (Southland) **Description** Medium-sized to large, equivalve, edentulous (lacking hinge teeth), elongate, oblong, inflated shells with a posterior gape **Original shell** Aragonite; usually preserved as thin grey to black films **Habitat** Shallow water, infaunal, deep burrowing in sand and silt **Diet** Suspension-feeding on plankton and organic matter **Notes** *Myonia* and its relatives (14 are recorded from New Zealand) are relatively common in some formations; they resemble modern *Zenatia* but are much more inflated. (1 cm)

Whole shell with left valve to camera

Streblochondria flexuosa

Phylum Mollusca **Class** Bivalvia **Family** Streblochondriidae **Age** Middle Permian YAr–YAf (273.0–260.4 Ma) **Rock units** Productus Creek Group (Southland) **Description** Small to medium equant shells with a rounded outline, weak inflation and obvious ears; ornament of strong commarginal growth lines and prominent wavy (hence *flexuosa*), round-crested radial ribs (costae) **Original shell** Calcite and aragonite **Habitat** Probably attached to the substrate by a byssus **Diet** Filter-feeding on plankton and suspended organic matter **Notes** More than 10 *Streblochondria* species are recorded from New Zealand Permian formations; they resemble modern limids. (5 mm)

Internal mould of right valve

Carpolithus mackayi

Kingdom Plantae **Order** Unknown **Age** Middle–Late Triassic Gk–Bw (238.5–204.6 Ma) **Rock units** Richmond Group (Wairoa Gorge near Nelson), Torlesse Supergroup (Tank Gully, Canterbury; Long Gully; near Benmore Dam) **Description** Ovate seed, slightly pointed at one end, rounded at the other, *c.*11.5 mm long by 8 mm wide, with a thicker central body surrounded by a thinner rim; the central body has a distinct median longitudinal groove **Notes** Thought to be the seed of a woody gymnosperm; possibly associated with *Linguifolium* (see p. 38). (5 mm)

Ginkgophytopsis lacerata

Kingdom Plantae **Order** Ginkgoales **Age** Middle–Late Triassic Gk–Bo (238.5–199.6 Ma) **Rock units** Torlesse Supergroup (Tank Gully and Benmore Dam, Canterbury; Long Gully, North Otago), Murihiku Supergroup (several localities) **Description** Leaves wedge-shaped, apical margin deeply incised; the veins extend upwards from the base, are subparallel and fork into two **Notes** Ginkgoales were widespread, distinctive and unusual plants; they first appeared in the Permian; most diverse in the Jurassic and Early Cretaceous; they disappear from the New Zealand fossil record in the Late Cretaceous; only one species still exists (in China) and is very similar to its Mesozoic ancestors. (1 cm)

Dicroidium odontopteroides var. *argenteum*

Kingdom Plantae **Order** Corystospermales **Age** Middle Triassic Gk (238.5–227.5 Ma) **Rock units** Torlesse Supergroup (Tank Gully, Canterbury) **Description** *Dicroidium* species have a singly forked rachis and are pinnate or bipinnate; this species is pinnate with subcircular or subrhombic pinnae, and the bases of the pinnae are constricted **Notes** *Dicroidium* is an extinct pteridosperm; these were seed plants that bore pollen-producing organs and seeds attached to their mostly fern-like foliage; pteridosperms first appeared in the Devonian and had almost disappeared by the Cenozoic; some Paleozoic groups were probably ancestral to modern conifers. (1 cm)

Linguifolium lilleanum

Kingdom Plantae **Order** Unknown **Age** Middle–Late Triassic Gk–Bo (238.5–199.6 Ma) **Rock units** Torlesse Supergroup (Tank Gully and Benmore Dam, Canterbury; Long Gully, North Otago), Taringatura Group (Otamita Stream, Southland and Highfield, Nelson) **Description** Simple leaves with smooth margins, 21–35 mm wide, lanceolate to obovate; apex subacute to rounded; base very acute; midrib narrower at apical end of leaf; secondary veins closely spaced, depart midvein at very acute angle and arch up and outwards **Notes** *Linguifolium* is a gymnosperm of uncertain affinity restricted to Middle to Late Triassic rocks. (1 cm)

Torlessia mackayi

Phylum Protista **Order** Foraminiferida **Family** Bathysiphonidae **Age** Middle–Late Triassic Gk–Bm (238.5–212.0 Ma) **Rock units** Torlesse Supergroup, Rakaia Terrane (North Otago, inland Canterbury, Wellington), Taringatura Group (Southland) **Description** Slender, tapering, slightly curved, cylindrical tube fossils; pale grey to white; smooth; commonly squashed with deformation fractures along tube length; tube comparatively thick; 20–60 mm long, up to 5 mm wide **Original shell** Agglutinated mineral grains **Habitat** Semi-infaunal, sticking upright in soft seafloor in deep water **Diet** Filter-feeding on plankton and suspended organic matter **Notes** The most common fossil in 'the greywacke'; an agglutinating foraminifera. (1 cm)

Fissirhynchia wakefieldensis

Phylum Brachiopoda **Class** Articulata **Family** Rhynchonellidae **Age** Late Triassic Br (227.5–217 0 Ma) **Rock units** Taringatura Group (Southland), Richmond Group (Nelson), Newcastle Group (SW Auckland) **Description** Medium-sized, triangular-ribbed, impunctate brachiopods; fully ribbed with numerous regular, radiating, sharp crests and deep furrows; rounded triangular outline; ventral valve with indistinct sulcus; fine ornament of commarginal growth lines; 10–25 mm in length **Original shell** Calcite **Habitat** Attached to substrate by pedicle in shallow water

Internal mould of dorsal valve

Diet Filter-feeding on plankton and suspended organic matter **Notes** *Fissirhynchia* includes four species; known only from Late Triassic rocks in New Zealand. (5 mm)

Ventral valve (above) and internal mould of ventral valve (below)

Phylum Brachiopoda **Class** Articulata **Family** Athyridae **Age** Late Triassic Bo (204.6–199.6 Ma) **Rock units** Taringatura Group (Southland), Richmond Group (Nelson), Newcastle Group (SW Auckland) **Description** Medium-sized, impunctate, equivalve shells with a distinctive straight hinge-line; prominent sulcus with two bounding radial ridges; smooth except for fine commarginal growth lines; 30–60 mm in length **Original shell** Calcite **Habitat** Attached to substrate by pedicle in shallow water **Diet** Filter-feeding on plankton and suspended organic matter **Notes** Shellbed-forming; probably the most common brachiopod in Late Triassic rocks in New Zealand; an indicator fossil for the Otapirian Stage (Bo). (1 cm)

Alipunctifera kaihikuana

Phylum Brachiopoda **Class** Articulata **Family** Spiriferinidae **Age** Middle Triassic Gk (238.5–227.5 Ma) **Rock units** North Range Group (Southland), Torlesse Supergroup (N Otago) **Description** Medium-sized, punctate, thick-shelled with a long, prominent hinge-line, prominent sulcus and strong, rounded radial ribs; wing-shaped outline, longer than high; 30–60 mm in length **Original shell** Calcite **Habitat** Attached to substrate by pedicle in shallow water **Diet** Filter-feeding on plankton and suspended organic matter **Notes** Shellbed-forming; this is probably the most common Middle Triassic brachiopod in New Zealand; it defines the base of the Kaihikuan Stage (Gk). (5 mm)

Internal moulds of ventral valve (above) and dorsal valve (below)

Mentzelia kawhiana

Internal mould of ventral valve

Phylum Brachiopoda **Class** Articulata **Family** Spiriferinidae **Age** Late Triassic Bo (204.6–199.6 Ma) **Rock units** Taringatura Group (Southland), Richmond Group (Nelson), Newcastle Group (SW Auckland) **Description** Medium-sized, length 20–50 mm, punctate, thick-shelled with an equant subcircular outline; hinge-line less than width of shell; weak, broad sulcus and low, rounded radial ribs; spinose ornament **Original shell** Calcite **Habitat** Attached to substrate by pedicle in shallow water **Diet** Filter-feeding on plankton and suspended organic matter **Notes** Easily recognised: one of only two spiriferinids in rocks of latest Triassic in New Zealand. (1 cm)

Mentzeliopsis parki

Phylum Brachiopoda **Class** Articulata **Family** Spiriferinidae **Age** Middle Triassic Gk (238.5–227.5 Ma) **Rock units** North Range Group (Southland), Torlesse Supergroup (N Otago) **Description** Medium-sized, length 20–50 mm, punctate, thick-shelled with prominent umbones; straight hinge-line shorter than shell width; outline subrounded to quadrate; prominent broad sulcus with strong rounded, curving radial ribs; ornament of relatively dense short spines **Original shell** Calcite **Habitat** Attached to substrate by pedicle in shallow water **Diet** Filter-feeding on plankton and suspended organic matter **Notes** Very distinctive because of its spinose outer surface; often with other brachiopods in Kaihikuan shell-beds. (1 cm)

Internal mould of ventral valve

Rastelligera acutissima

External mould and cast of ventral valve

Internal mould of ventral valve

Phylum Brachiopoda **Class** Articulata **Family** Spiriferinidae **Age** Late Triassic Bo (204.6–199.6 Ma) **Rock units** Taringatura Group (Southland), Richmond Group (Nelson), Newcastle Group (SW Auckland) **Description** Medium-sized, length 40–80 mm, punctate, thick-shelled; long, prominent, distinctive hinge-line bearing a rastellum; prominent sulcus; strong rounded radial ribs; elongate wing shape; much longer than high **Original shell** Calcite **Habitat** Attached by pedicle in shallow water; often found in sandstone **Diet** Filter-feeding on plankton and suspended organic matter **Notes** Very distinctive and handsome spiriferinid; about 10 species have been recognised in New Zealand. (1 cm)

Sisenna hectori

Internal mould (top)

Phylum Mollusca **Class** Gastropoda **Family** Raphistomatidae **Age** Late Triassic Br (227.5–217.0 Ma) **Rock units** Taringatura Group (Southland), Richmond Group (Nelson), Newcastle Group (SW Auckland) **Description** Medium-sized, width 20–40 mm, thick-shelled squat snails; broad, flattened spire and compressed whorls; ornament of conspicuous knobs or ribs, radial threads and commarginal growth lines **Original shell** Aragonite **Habitat** Shallow water shelf environments **Diet** Probably herbivorous, grazing on algae **Notes** Probably the most common gastropod found in Late Triassic rocks of New Zealand; as with many aragonitic shells in New Zealand Mesozoic rocks, the original shell alters to chlorite, a soft green-black mineral. (1 cm)

Manticula problematica

Phylum Mollusca **Class** Bivalvia **Family** Mytilidae **Age** Late Triassic Bm (217.0–212.0 Ma) **Rock units** Taringatura Group (Southland), Richmond Group (Nelson), Newcastle Group (SW Auckland), Torlesse Supergroup (Rakaia Terrane, inland Canterbury) **Description** Medium-sized to large, length 50–150 mm, inequivalve, smooth clams; inflated left valve; much flatter right valve; rounded obliquely ovate, mussel-shaped; lumpy-looking shells (left valves rather like paua) with irregular weak growth stops **Original shell** Calcite **Habitat** Inner shelf to midshelf; opportunistic and gregarious on soft substrates **Diet** Filter-feeding on plankton **Notes** Very distinctive; shellbed-forming; defines the base of the Otamitan Stage (Bm). (1 cm)

Internal mould of left valve

Halobia cf. *hoernesi*

Phylum Mollusca **Class** Bivalvia **Family** Halobiidae **Age** Late Triassic Br (227.5–217.0 Ma) **Rock units** North Range Group (Southland), Torlesse Supergroup (Rakaia Terrane, inland Canterbury; Waipapa Terrane, Northland) **Description** Small to medium-sized, length 15–45 mm, equivalve, thin-shelled flat clams; hinge-line long, straight; with auricle and byssal tube; rounded subcircular outline; strong regular, radial ornament; weaker commarginal lines **Original shell** Calcite **Habitat** Marine shelf environments; opportunistic gregarious clams; attached to substrate by a byssus **Diet** Filter-feeding on plankton **Notes** Evolved from *Daonella*; widespread in Late Triassic seas; more than eight species known from New Zealand Triassic rocks. (1 cm)

Internal mould of right valve

Monotis (Entomonotis) richmondiana acutecostata

Phylum Mollusca **Class** Bivalvia **Family** Monotidae (bivalve) **Age** Late Triassic Bw (212.0–204.6 Ma) **Rock units** Taringatura Group (Southland), Richmond Group (Nelson), Newcastle Group (SW Auckland), Torlesse Supergroup (inland Canterbury, inland Kapiti Coast) **Description** Distinctive medium-sized, inequivalve clams with variable radial ribs and commarginals; auricle supported a byssus for attachment to substrate, rather like modern mussels **Original shell** Calcite **Habitat** Inner shelf to midshelf; gregarious, forming shellbeds **Diet** Filter-feeding on plankton **Notes** Several genera and subgenera and more than 12 species are recognised; *Monotis* means 'single ear'; *Monotis* defines the base of the Warepan Stage (Bw). (1 cm)

Internal mould of left valve

Otapiria dissimilis

Phylum Mollusca **Class** Bivalvia **Family** Monotidae (bivalve) **Age** Late Triassic Bo (204.6–199.6 Ma) **Rock units** Taringatura Group (Southland), Richmond Group (Nelson), Newcastle Group (SW Auckland), Torlesse Supergroup (inland Canterbury) **Description** Small to medium-sized, length 15–60 mm, inequivalve clams; thin-shelled; obliquely ovate; numerous regular, fine radial threads on inflated left valve; smooth, flatter right valve **Original shell** Calcite **Habitat** Inner shelf to midshelf; gregarious; probably attached by a byssus **Diet** Filter-feeding on plankton **Notes** An opportunistic clam that forms shellbeds; at least four forms of *Otapiria* are present in Late Triassic–Early Jurassic rocks of New Zealand. (1 cm)

Internal mould of left valve with some shell

Amphipopanoceras fraseri

Phylum Mollusca **Class** Cephalopoda **Subclass** Ammonoidea **Family** Parapopanoceratidae **Age** Middle Triassic Ge (244.5–238.5 Ma) **Rock units** North Range Group (Southland) **Description** Width 15–50 mm, small, globose and moderately involute ammonoids with a small, deep umbilicus and a smooth shell, lacking ornament; distinctive simple ceratitic suture pattern **Original shell** Aragonite **Habitat** Pelagic marine shelf environments **Diet** Crustaceans, fish and small invertebrates **Notes** This ammonoid is known from just a few localities in Southland; usually crushed; notably preserved within mud-balls at one locality; the most common ammonoid known from Middle Triassic rocks of New Zealand. (1 cm)

Rhacophyllites debilis

Phylum Mollusca **Class** Cephalopoda **Subclass** Ammonoidea **Family** Discophyllitidae **Age** Late Triassic Bm (217.0–212.0 Ma) **Rock units** Taringatura Group (Southland), Richmond Group (Nelson), Newcastle Group (SW Auckland), Torlesse Supergroup (inland Canterbury) **Description** Medium-sized to large, width 100–500 mm, evolute, smooth ammonoids; distinctive suture pattern; fine, regular growth lines **Original shell** Aragonite **Habitat** Pelagic marine shelf environments **Diet** Crustaceans, fish and small invertebrates **Notes** Known from many fragmentary fossils, mainly as internal moulds of inner whorls; large size and distinctive suture permit easy identification; most common ammonoid from Late Triassic rocks of New Zealand. (5 cm)

Internal mould of inner whorls revealing suture pattern

Cladophlebis sp.

Kingdom Plantae **Family** Osmundaceae **Age** Triassic to Cretaceous (251–65.5 Ma) **Rock units** Murihiku and Torlesse Supergroups, many localities: Curio Bay, Hokonui Hills, Mataura Falls (Southland); Malvern Hills, Clent Hills (Canterbury); and Waikato Heads (Auckland); the illustrated specimen is from Malvern Hills **Description** Bipinnate frond; pinnules variable in size with entire margins; attach straight onto the rachis; venation of strong midvein with lateral veins that split in style of a tuning fork **Notes** *Cladophlebis* is a name applied to infertile bipinnate fern foliage; common and widespread in the Mesozoic; referred to as the 'great weed of Mesozoic times'. (5 cm)

Ptilophyllum acutifolium

Kingdom Plantae **Order** Bennettitales **Age** Middle Jurassic Kt (175.6–157.5 Ma) **Rock units** Ferndale Group, Murihiku Supergroup (Curio Bay, Southland) **Description** Pinnate leaf; the pinnules have acute apices, are broadest at their base (*c*. 3 mm), and are arranged alternately along the rachis; the veins are subparallel, originate from the pinnule base and extend to the apex. **Notes** The Bennettitales are an extinct coniferous group which resembled the modern cycads. (5 cm)

Aucklandirhynchia sexagesimae

Phylum Brachiopoda **Class** Articulata **Family** Rhynchonellidae **Age** Early Jurassic Hu (188.0–175.6 Ma) **Rock units** Newcastle Group (SW Auckland), Taringatura Group (Southland) **Description** Small to medium-sized, length 10–12 mm; shells with rounded to triangular outline; ventral valve with distinct rounded sulcus; costae strong, rounded; beak large with large circular foramen **Original shell** Calcite **Habitat** Attached to substrate by pedicle in shallow water **Diet** Filter-feeding on plankton and suspended organic matter

Notes Usually found in sandstones, suggesting a preference for higher energy environments; over five forms recognised in Early to Middle Jurassic formations. (1 cm)

External mould of ventral valve (upper) and internal mould of dorsal valve (lower)

Sakawairhynchia bartrumi

Phylum Brachiopoda **Class** Articulata **Family** Rhynchonellidae **Age** Early Jurassic Ha–Hu (199.5–175.6 Ma) **Rock units** Newcastle Group (SW Auckland), Taringatura Group (Southland) **Description** Medium-sized, length 10–18 mm; shells with rounded triangular to pentagonal or elliptical outline; well-inflated; brachial valve more inflated and plicate; smooth posterior, 3–10 bluntly rounded costae to anterior, more on brachial valve **Original shell** Calcite **Habitat** Attached to

Internal mould of dorsal valve

substrate by pedicle in shallow water **Diet** Filter-feeding on plankton and suspended organic matter **Notes** Usually found in sandstones, suggesting a preference for higher energy environments; over 13 forms are recognised in New Zealand but only three are Jurassic. (1 cm)

Phylum Mollusca **Class** Bivalvia **Family** Buchiidae **Age** Late Jurassic Ko–Op (153.5–145.5 Ma) **Rock units** Rengarenga Group (SW Auckland) **Description** Medium-sized, length 30–90 mm, obliquely elongate, inequivalve shells; inflated left valve and a much flatter right valve; commonly with a prominent growth stop and twisted and highly curved beak on the left valve **Original shell** Calcite **Habitat** Epifaunal; attached to the substrate by a byssus; shallow water; opportunistic, gregarious, shellbed-forming **Diet** Filter-feeding on plankton and suspended organic matter **Notes** One of more than seven species from the Puaroan Stage (Op), spanning 3 million years of latest Jurassic time. (1 cm)

Pseudaucella marshalli

Phylum Mollusca **Class** Bivalvia **Family** Buchiidae **Age** Early Jurassic Hu (188.0–175.6 Ma) **Rock units** Newcastle Group (SW Auckland), Taringatura Group (Southland) **Description** Small to medium-sized, length 10–40 mm, inflated, equivalve, subtriangular shells; smooth with strong growth stops, especially near shell margin; pronounced sulcus on both valves **Original shell** Calcite **Habitat** Epifaunal; attached to the substrate by a short byssus; opportunistic gregarious shells occurring in shallow water **Diet** Filter-feeding on plankton and suspended organic matter **Notes** Shellbed-forming; this fossil defines the base of the Ururoan Stage (Hu); one of 11 buchiids known from New Zealand Jurassic rocks. (1 cm)

Retroceramus inconditus

Internal moulds

Phylum Mollusca **Class** Bivalvia **Family** Retroceramidae **Age** Middle Jurassic Kt (175.6–157.5 Ma) **Rock units** Newcastle Group (SW Auckland) **Description** Medium-sized to large, length 60–150 mm, inequilateral clams, equivalve, elongate mussel-shaped and moderately globose with ornament of weak, irregular corrugations **Original shell** Calcite and aragonite; outer shell of distinctive prismatic calcite (like horse mussels) **Habitat** Epifaunal; attached to the substrate by a short byssus **Diet** Filter-feeding on plankton and suspended organic matter; may have had symbiotic algae **Notes** Ancestral to the younger *Retroceramus galoi* (see entry below); best preserved in siltstone. (1 cm)

Retroceramus galoi

Phylum Mollusca **Class** Bivalvia **Family** Retroceramidae **Age** Late Jurassic Kh (157.5–153.5 Ma) **Rock units** Newcastle Group (SW Auckland) **Description** Medium-sized to large, length 40–120 mm, inequilateral clams, equivalve, obliquely ovate, moderately globose; prominent beaks; strong, rounded regular corrugations **Original shell** Calcite and aragonite; outer shell of distinctive prismatic calcite (like horse mussels) **Habitat** Epifaunal; attached to the substrate by a short byssus **Diet** Filter-feeding on plankton and suspended organic matter; may have had symbiotic algae **Notes** More than 12 species of *Retroceramus* are known from New Zealand Jurassic rocks; this form defines the base of the Heterian Stage (Kh). (1 cm)

Calliphylloceras empedoclis

Phylum Mollusca **Class** Cephalopoda **Subclass** Ammonoidea **Family** Phylloceratidae **Age** Late Jurassic Ko–Op (153.5–145.5 Ma) **Rock units** Rengarenga Group (SW Auckland) **Description** Width 80–250 mm, smooth, involute, disc-shaped; fewer than seven shallow constrictions (growth stops) per whorl; ornamented with fine, thread-like lirae that are straight or slightly curved and never bundled; small umbilicus **Original shell** Aragonite **Habitat** Pelagic marine shelf environments **Diet** Crustaceans, fish and small invertebrates **Notes** This specimen has superb suture patterns, ornate architectural features that develop where the septae meet the tubular whorl of the shell. (1 cm)

Lytoceras taharoaense

Phylum Mollusca **Class** Cephalopoda **Subclass** Ammonoidea **Family** Lytoceratidae **Age** Late Jurassic Kh (157.5–153.5 Ma) **Rock units** Rengarenga Group (SW Auckland) **Description** Medium-sized to large ammonites, width 65–120 mm; evolute, serpenticone shells with regular, close-spaced, crenulated ribs or growth lines (resembling an elephant's trunk) and some conspicuous growth stops **Original shell** Aragonite **Habitat** Pelagic marine environments **Diet** Crustaceans, fish and small invertebrates **Notes** This species is famous for its giants, up to 1500 mm in width; New Zealand boasts the largest known Jurassic ammonite (larger ammonites of Cretaceous age are recorded from elsewhere). (5 cm)

Aspidoceras cf. *euomphaloides*

Phylum Mollusca **Class** Ammonoidea **Family** Aspidoceratidae **Age** Late Jurassic Kh (157.5–153.5 Ma) **Rock units** Rengarenga Group (SW Auckland) **Description** Width 40–65 mm, globose ammonite; rounded whorls with two rows of tubercles, the outer row placed near the middle of the whorl and fading in strength with growth, the inner composed of small, dense, spinous tubercles which broaden into gentle folds with growth; fine growth lines **Original shell** Aragonite **Habitat** Pelagic marine shelf environments **Diet** Crustaceans, fish and small invertebrates **Notes** This ammonite is known from just a few localities in the Kawhia Harbour region. (1 cm)

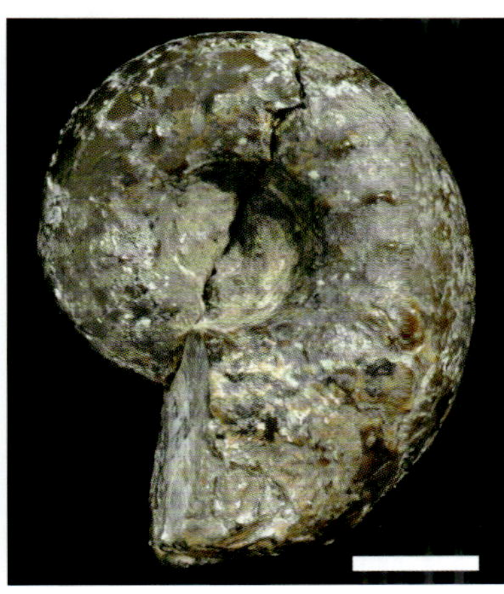

Aulacosphinctoides brownei

Phylum Mollusca **Class** Cephalopoda **Subclass** Ammonoidea **Family** Ataxioceratidae **Age** Late Jurassic Op (148.5–145.5 Ma) **Rock units** Rengarenga Group (SW Auckland) **Description** Width 50–120 mm, planulate, evolute; regularly spaced and well-defined sharp, straight ribs on inner whorls; ribs equally regular and sharp on the outer whorls but most bifurcate about two-thirds up the whorl flanks; up to four irregularly spaced constrictions (growth stops) are present on each whorl **Original shell** Aragonite **Habitat** Pelagic marine shelf environments **Diet** Crustaceans, fish and small invertebrates **Notes** This is a classic-looking ammonite, like a coiled snake-like tube. (1 cm)

Kossmatia cf. *desmidoptycha*

Phylum Mollusca **Class** Cephalopoda **Subclass** Ammonoidea **Family** Ataxioceratidae **Age** Late Jurassic Ko (153.5–148.5 Ma) **Rock units** Rengarenga Group (SW Auckland) **Description** Width 65–120 mm, ribbed, evolute; high outer whorl; conspicuous sharp, regular, rounded ribs that are fasciculate and wavy with an elongate S shape **Original shell** Aragonite **Habitat** Pelagic marine shelf environments **Diet** Crustaceans, fish and small invertebrates **Notes** More than 12 species of *Kossmatia* occur within 2500 m of sedimentary rock in the Kawhia Harbour area. (1 cm)

External mould (left) and internal mould (right)

Belemnopsis aucklandica

Phylum Mollusca **Class** Cephalopoda **Family** Belemnopseidae **Age** Late Jurassic Op (148.3–145.5 Ma) **Rock units** Rengarenga Group (SW Auckland) **Description** Elongate, bullet-shaped with a pointed, bulbous end and a hollow, tapering posterior end;

groove or furrow down the ventral side **Original shell** Calcite; they served as internal 'shell' structures (like divers' weight-belts) for an extinct group of squid **Habitat** Pelagic open ocean environments **Diet** Crustaceans, fish, other invertebrates **Notes** Belemnites preserve extremely well; distinctive radiating structure in cross-section; two belemnite genera (*Belemnopsis*, *Hibolithes*) and more than 25 species are recorded from New Zealand Jurassic rocks; this species is an indicator fossil for the Puaroan Stage. (1 cm)

Araucarioxylon novaezeelandiae

Kingdom Plantae **Family** Araucariaceae **Age** Late Cretaceous Mp (86.5–83.5 Ma) **Rock units** Okarahia Sandstone (Haumuri Bluff, Marlborough) **Description** Wood; short section of a small petrified tree trunk with growth rings visible; the diagnostic features which distinguish this wood from other coniferous woods are visible only in thin sections viewed under a microscope **Notes** Petrification of wood involves the replacement of the original wood with minerals; the original wood here has been replaced by silica in the inner

part and carbonate in the outer part; this specimen was famously described by Marie Stopes in 1914. (5 cm)

Araucaria haastii

Kingdom Plantae **Family** Araucariaceae **Age** Late Cretaceous Mh (83.5–65.5 Ma) **Rock units** Taratu Formation (Shag Point, Otago; Malvern Hills, Canterbury), Rewanui Member of the Paparoa Coal Measures (Strongman Mine, Greymouth), Maungataniwha Sandstone (Hawke's Bay) **Description** Moderately narrow, arched leaf; acute apex; blunt, stem-clasping base; lacking a midrib; distinctive fine, parallel venation; sometimes found as several leaves closely and spirally attached to stems **Notes** The Araucariaceae family was diverse in Mesozoic time; araucarian foliage and cone scales are common in New Zealand Jurassic and Cretaceous rocks; there are three living araucarian genera (*Araucaria*, *Agathis*, *Wollemia*),

but only one species *Agathis australis* (kauri) occurs naturally in the modern New Zealand flora. (1 cm)

Podocarp foliage and broadleaf (dicotyledonous) angiosperm leaf base

Kingdom Plantae **Family** Podocarpaceae; angiosperm unassigned **Age** Late Cretaceous Mh (83.5–65.5 Ma) **Rock units** Rewanui Member of the Paparoa Coal Measures (Greymouth) **Description** Podocarp leaves 5–8 mm in length and *c.* 1 mm wide, arranged alternately; individual leaves have a strong midvein **Notes** Small-leaved conifer foliage of this type with a midvein visible on the leaves is often assumed to belong to the Podocarpaceae; podocarp foliage fragments are common in Cretaceous leaf assemblages. (5 cm)

Broadleaf angiosperm (left); podocarp foliage (right)

'Patete scheffleri'

Kingdom Plantae **Family** Unknown **Age** Late Cretaceous Mh (83.5–65.5 Ma) **Rock units** Pakawau Group (NW Nelson) **Description** A simple angiosperm leaf with attenuate apex, broad rounded base and serrate margin; the secondary veins are straight to curved and irregularly spaced **Notes** This specimen was collected

by James Hector in 1868 and illustrated beautifully, although not published; there is some uncertainty over its collection locality, but colouring of the specimen and matrix is more like that of the Cretaceous Pakawau Group than overlying Paleocene Farewell Formation. (5 cm)

Notidanodon dentatus

Phylum Chordata **Class** Chondrichthyes **Family** Hexanchidae **Age** Late Cretaceous Mp–Mh (86.5–65.5 Ma) **Rock units** Tinui Group (Hawke's Bay), Eyre Group (SE Marlborough–N Canterbury) **Description** Comb-like row of flattened, inclined, blade-shaped teeth, with individual teeth largest in the centre of the 'comb' and diminishing in size on either side **Original material** Enamel (apatite) **Habitat** Marine; living species spend most of their lives in the deep ocean **Diet** Fish **Notes** Hexanchids include the primitive cow sharks with up to seven pairs of gill slits (in contrast to five in most sharks); this fossil shark had comb-like teeth along the lower jaw only. (1 cm)

Moanasaurus mangahouangae

Phylum Chordata **Class** Reptilia **Family** Mosasauridae **Age** Late Cretaceous Mh (83.5–65.5 Ma) **Rock units** Tinui Group (Hawke's Bay) **Description** Part of the upper jaw of a large marine reptile; teeth slightly curved, conical, with flattened, oval cross-sections, sharp front and rear edges, and distinctive faceted crowns **Original material** Enamel (apatite) and bone **Habitat** Marine, open ocean; air-breathing **Diet** Almost anything! **Notes** Mosasaurs had crocodile-like bodies, flattened tails and short, paddle-shaped limbs;

length up to 17 m; *Moanasaurus mangahouangae* was 'only' about 12 m; top marine predators in Late Cretaceous time following extinction of ichthyosaurs and pliosaurs; related to monitor lizards; they had two extra rows of teeth at the back of the mouth, ensuring no escape for prey. (5 cm)

Rotularia sp.

Phylum Annelida **Class** Polychaeta **Family** Serpulidae **Subfamily** Spirorbinae **Age** Late Cretaceous Mh (70.6–65.5 Ma) **Rock units** Widespread in Late Cretacous rocks of New Zealand, Pitt Island Group (Chatham Islands) **Description** Width 10–30 mm, irregular, small to medium-sized, coiled tubes expanding with age; often turbinoform, resembling a gastropod, with irregular, scaly surface of commarginal growth lines **Original shell** Calcite **Habitat** Shallow marine, attached to shell or rock substrates **Diet** Carnivorous or omnivorous; anything organic **Notes** Few 'worms' produce a skeletal structure or in this case a tube; similar in lifestyle to much smaller, more regularly coiled smooth-shelled *Spirorbis*. (1 cm)

Inoceramus australis

Phylum Mollusca **Class** Bivalvia **Family** Inoceramidae **Age** Late Cretaceous Mp (86.5–83.5 Ma) **Rock units** Widespread in Northland Allochthon (Northland), Matawai and Ruatoria Groups (Raukumara), Mangapurupuru Group and Glenburn Formation (Wairarapa), Hapuku and Seymour Groups (Marlborough) **Description** Large clam, length up to 20 cm, inequilateral, equivalve; large and regularly spaced commarginal folds **Original shell** Calcite and aragonite **Habitat** Marine, shallow to deep water; epifaunal, possibly attached by a byssus **Diet** Filter-feeding on plankton and suspended organic matter **Notes** Restricted to the New Zealand Piripauan Stage. (5 cm)

Cremnoceramus bicorrugatus bicorrugatus

Phylum Mollusca **Class** Bivalvia **Family** Inoceramidae **Age** Late Cretaceous Rm (93.0–88.6 Ma) **Rock units** Matawai and Ruatoria Groups (Raukumara), Glenburn Formation (Wairarapa), Hapuku Group (Marlborough) **Description** Large clam, length over 40 cm; inequilateral, inequivalve; fairly regular commarginal ribs superimposed on large, rather irregular commarginal folds; dramatic change in shape (geniculation) at about 10 cm such that juvenile shell looks bulbous **Original shell** Calcite and aragonite **Habitat** Marine, relatively shallow to deep water; epifaunal; juvenile shells attached by a byssus **Diet** Filter-feeding on plankton and suspended organic matter **Notes** Restricted to the New Zealand Mangaotanean Stage. (5 cm)

Magadiceramus rangatira rangatira

Fragment of shell surface   *Cross section of shell fragments*

Phylum Mollusca **Class** Bivalvia **Family** Inoceramidae **Age** Late Cretaceous Ra (95.2–93.0 Ma) **Rock units** Widespread in Northland Allochthon (Northland), Tinui and Ruatoria Groups (Raukumara), Glenburn Formation (Wairarapa), and Seymour and Hapuku Groups (Marlborough) **Description** Gigantic clam over 1.5 m long; inequilateral and inequivalve; oval outline; large commarginal folds; distinctive ornament of fine, radial wrinkles criss-cross each other; outer shell of fibrous ('prismatic') calcite over 1 cm thick **Original shell** Calcite and aragonite **Habitat** Marine, living at relatively shallow depths to deep water; epifaunal **Diet** Filter-feeding on plankton and suspended organic matter **Notes** This common species is one of the largest clams ever to have existed. (5 cm, 1 cm)

Aucellina euglypha

Phylum Mollusca **Class** Bivalvia **Family** Buchiidae **Age** Early Cretaceous Cm (103.3–100.2 Ma) **Rock units** Northland Allochthon (Northland), Matawai Group (Raukumara), Mangapurupuru Group (Wairarapa), Coverham and Wallow Groups (Marlborough) **Description** Small, thin-shelled, inequilateral, inequivalve clam; inflated, bulbous left valve and almost flat right valve; most specimens with sculpture of very fine radial ribs **Original shell** Calcite and aragonite **Habitat** Marine, moderately deep water at outer shelf; epifaunal, attached by a byssus **Diet** Filter-feeding on plankton and suspended organic matter **Notes** Can form massive shellbeds containing just the single species; used to recognise the base of the New Zealand Motuan Stage. (1 cm)

Entolium membranaceum

Phylum Mollusca **Class** Bivalvia **Family** Entoliidae **Age** Late Cretaceous Mp–Mh (86.5–65.5 Ma) **Rock units** Northland Allochthon (Northland), Tinui Group (Raukumara and Hawke's Bay), Seymour and Eyre Groups (Marlborough–Canterbury), Kahuitara Tuff (Chatham Islands) **Description** Small, equilateral, equivalve clam; two approximately equal auricles; shell thin, smooth with very fine and regularly spaced commarginal lines **Original shell** Calcite and aragonite **Habitat** Marine, epifaunal, probably able to swim like scallops **Diet** Filter-feeding on plankton and suspended organic matter **Notes** Common in New Zealand Late Cretaceous shallow marine formations, and the same species is known from rocks of this age all around the world. (1 cm)

Iotrigonia glyptica

Phylum Mollusca **Class** Bivalvia **Family** Trigoniidae **Age** Early Cretaceous Cn–Ra (100.2–93.0 Ma) **Rock units** Matawai Group (Raukumara Peninsula), Glenburn Formation (Wairarapa), Bluff Sandstone (Marlborough) **Description** Broad, wing-shaped clam of medium size; distinctive radial ribs that converge in a V-shaped pattern on the anterior third of shell **Original shell** Aragonite **Habitat** Marine, buried within sand **Diet** Filter-feeding on plankton and suspended organic matter **Notes** The trigoniid clams were abundant during the Mesozoic; only a handful of species live around Australia today; the ridges on the shell helped them burrow rapidly through shifting sand. (1 cm)

Pterotrigonia pseudocaudata

Phylum Mollusca **Class** Bivalvia **Family** Trigoniidae **Age** Late Cretaceous Mp–?Mh (86.5–?65.5 Ma) **Rock units** Widespread in Northland Allochthon (Northland), Tinui Group (Raukumara and Hawke's Bay), Seymour and Eyre Groups (Marlborough–Canterbury), Kahuitara Tuff (Chatham Islands), Onekakara Group (Otago) **Description** Small to medium-sized clam, equivalve, quite highly inflated, strongly inequilateral; covered with strong, nodose, radial ribs that become progressively weaker over the extended posterior part of the shell **Original shell** Aragonite **Habitat** Marine, buried within sand **Diet** Filter-feeding on plankton and suspended organic matter **Notes** Trigoniid clams like *Pterotrigonia pseudocaudata* and *Iotrigonia glyptica* (see above entry) underwent rapid evolution so that there is a great profusion of Cretaceous species. (1 cm)

Eriphyla meridiana

Phylum Mollusca **Class** Bivalvia **Family** Astartidae **Age** Late Cretaceous Mp–Mh (86.5–65.5 Ma) **Rock units** Tinui Group (Raukumara and Hawke's Bay), Seymour and Eyre Groups (Marlborough–Canterbury), Onekakara Group (Otago) **Description** Clam of small to medium size, almost circular outline, equivalve, with fine and numerous commarginal ribs **Original shell** Aragonite **Habitat** Marine, probably inner shelf to midshelf depths; infaunal

Diet Filter-feeding on plankton and suspended organic matter **Notes** One of the common infaunal clams in New Zealand Cretaceous shallow marine rocks. (1 cm)

Aphrodina (Tikia) wilckensi

Phylum Mollusca **Class** Bivalvia **Family** Veneridae **Age** Late Cretaceous Mp–Mh (86.5–65.5 Ma) **Rock units** Tinui Group (Raukumara and Hawke's Bay), Seymour Group (Marlborough–N Canterbury), Onekakara Group (Otago), Kahuitara Tuff (Chatham Islands)

Description Small to medium-sized, inequilateral, ovate, equivalve clams; weak to moderate commarginal ribs and growth lines **Original shell** Aragonite **Habitat** Marine, probably inner shelf to midshelf; infaunal with two siphon tubes, one tube drawing clean water into the shell and the other expelling waste water **Diet** Filter-feeding on plankton and suspended organic matter **Notes** One of the common infaunal clams in New Zealand Cretaceous shallow marine rocks. (1 cm)

Protodolium speighti

Phylum Mollusca **Class** Gastropoda **Family** Neritopsidae **Age** Late Cretaceous Mp–Mh (86.5–65.5 Ma) **Rock units** Northland Allochthon (Northland), Tinui Group (Hawke's Bay), Seymour and Eyre Groups (Marlborough–Canterbury), Onekakara Group (Otago) **Description** Snail of medium size, rather bulbous, with strong, smooth, raised and flat-topped spiral ribs; shell thick and robust **Original shell** Aragonite **Habitat** Shallow marine, epifaunal **Diet** Grazing on algae **Notes** *Protodolium* was apparently endemic to the south-west Pacific region during the Late Cretaceous; found only in New Zealand, New Caledonia, and the Chatham Islands (a different species); it is relatively common in New Zealand shallow marine Cretaceous rocks. (1 cm)

Conchothyra parasitica

Phylum Mollusca **Class** Gastropoda **Family** Struthiolariidae **Age** Late Cretaceous Mp–Ma (86.5–65.5 Mh) **Rock units** Seymour and Eyre Groups (Marlborough–Canterbury) **Description** Strange-looking! The adult shell is of medium size and enveloped entirely in a thick layer of secondary shell – the 'callus'; apart from growth lines, the shell has no sculpture or surface patterning **Original shell** Aragonite **Habitat** Shallow marine, semi-infaunal **Diet** Deposit-feeder, extracting organic particles from the sediment **Notes** Endemic to the New Zealand region; oldest member of the family Struthiolariidae, the living ostrich-foot shells; the reason for the massive thick shell is probably to resist attack from shell-crushing predators. (1 cm)

Dimitobelus superstes

Phylum Mollusca **Class** Cephalopoda **Family** Dimitobelidae **Age** Early–Late Cretaceous Cm–Rm (103.0–88.6 Ma) **Rock units** Northland Allochthon (Northland), Matawai Group (Raukumara), Mangapurupuru Group (Wairarapa), Coverham and Wallow Groups (Marlborough) **Description** Solid, bullet-shaped shell with oval cross-section, tapering to a point at one end, conical depression at the other end; two shallow grooves extend some distance from the blunt end; shell of radially arranged fibres **Original shell** Calcite **Habitat** Open marine **Diet** Small fish, crustaceans and probably other squids **Notes** Belemnites are the internal shells of an extinct type of squid; the solid shell or 'guard' was enclosed within the body near the tail of the animal. (1 cm)

Scaphites equalis coverhamensis

Phylum Mollusca **Class** Cephalopoda **Family** Scaphitidae **Age** Late Cretaceous Cn (100.2–95.2 Ma) **Rock units** East Coast Allochthon (Raukumara), Coverham Group (Marlborough) **Description** A curious small ammonite with the juvenile shell coiled in a flat spiral (as in most ammonites), but with a partially uncoiled adult shell

and the final growth stage curved back to form a hook; well-developed, regular ribs that become more widely spaced and coarser on the adult shell **Original shell** Aragonite **Habitat** Marine, open ocean **Diet** Crustaceans and small fish **Notes** Scaphitid ammonites were abundant and diverse during the Cretaceous; found globally; *Scaphites equalis* is the 'type species' – the species used to define the genus. (1 cm)

Vertebrites murdochi

Phylum Mollusca **Class** Cephalopoda **Family** Gaudryceratidae **Age** Late Cretaceous Mp–Mh (86.5–65.5 Ma) **Rock units** Northland Allochthon (Northland), Whangai Formation (Raukumara) **Description** Small with numerous squashed-looking whorls like a soft car tyre in cross-section; very fine, close-spaced ribs on sides of shell that angle towards aperture and fade over the venter **Original shell** Aragonite **Habitat** Marine, open ocean **Diet** Crustaceans and small fish **Notes** Like modern squid, ammonites swam using 'jet-propulsion'; like living *Nautilus*, they could also vary the amount of gas within chambers in the shell and use this to control their buoyancy and the depth at which they floated. (1 cm)

Kossmaticeras bensoni

Phylum Mollusca **Class** Cephalopoda **Family** Kossmaticeratidae **Age** Late Cretaceous Mp?–Mh (86.5?–65.5 Ma) **Rock units** Whangai Formation (Raukumara), Onekakara Group (Otago) **Description** Moderately large; each whorl has an oval cross-section; shell with numerous, relatively strong, sinuous, primary ribs that angle towards the aperture with a single, slightly finer secondary rib between each primary rib; for every three to five primary ribs, there is a raised, elongate bump; a few constrictions, parallel to the primary ribs, affect the outer whorl **Original shell** Aragonite **Habitat** Marine, open ocean **Diet** Crustaceans and small fish **Notes** For reasons that are not clear, ammonites are generally rare in New Zealand Cretaceous rocks. (5 cm)

Zoophycos sp.

Trace fossil **Age** Late Cretaceous to Eocene Mh–Ar (83.5–34.5 Ma) **Rock units** Muzzle Group (Marlborough) **Description** Length 5–100 mm, regular and/or irregular, well-defined or subtle, well-organised and/or repeated; this form has nested, U-shaped, curving, linear traces in the plane of strata; in three dimensions, it appears as a large auger spiralling through the strata **Original material** No skeletal material; traces due to burrowing activity of some organism **Habitat** *Zoophycos* is relatively common in fine-grained limestone, marl, mudstone and siltstone; deep water (over 150 m deep); the organism responsible was infaunal; probably an echinoderm **Diet** Suspension-feeding **Notes** Trace fossils are very common; can occur in any sedimentary rock; Ward Beach is famous for its smooth trace fossil-bearing pebbles and cobbles. (1 cm)

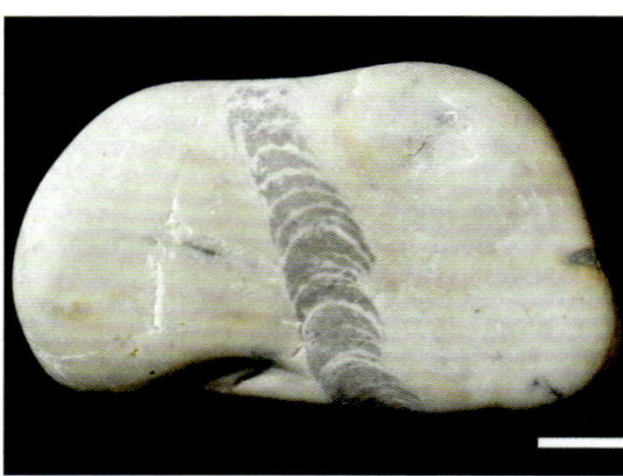

Paleodictyon sp.

Trace fossil **Age** Late Cretaceous to Eocene Mh–Ar (83.5–34.5 Ma) **Rock units** Tora Group (Wairarapa Coast) **Description** Highly organised; regular repeated, geometric, hexagonal structures resembling chicken-netting lying on the plane of strata; 50–150 mm in length **Original material** No skeletal material; traces due to activity of some organism **Habitat** Occurring in relatively deep marine mudstone and siltstone; over 150 m water depth **Diet** The organism responsible for this fossil is unknown; probably a worm; suspension feeding **Notes** This is a very distinctive trace fossil; not common but illustrates just how interesting the mysterious world of trace fossils can be. (5 cm)

Podocarp foliage

Kingdom Plantae **Family** Podocarpaceae **Age** Paleocene Dt
(65.5–55.8 Ma) **Rock units** Goldlight Mudstone (Greymouth)
Description Small sprig of podocarp leaves; individual leaves
are lanceolate to ovate in shape, have smooth margins, 4–8 mm
in length and *c.*1 mm wide; apices and bases are acute; a midvein
can be seen on several of the leaves; the leaves are sessile; appear
spirally arranged around the stem. (1 cm)

'Dryandra' comptoniaefolia

Kingdom Plantae **Family** Proteaceae **Age** Paleocene Dt (65.5–
55.8 Ma) **Rock units** Goldlight Mudstone (Greymouth), Broken
River Coal Measures (Cave Stream and S Canterbury), Farewell
Formation (NW Nelson) **Description** Long, narrow leaf; acute
apex and acute base; prominent teeth incising almost to the midvein
in some specimens; tooth shape is distinctive: usually straight on the
apical side, convex on the basal side; short secondary veins extend
into each tooth apex **Notes** This very distinctive angiosperm leaf is
only known from Paleocene rocks in New Zealand; proteaceans have
diverse and rich New Zealand fossil records yet only two species
remain: *Knightia excelsa* (rewarewa) and *Toronia toru* (toru). (1 cm)

'Cinnamomum' waikatoensis

Kingdom Plantae **Family** Lauraceae **Age** Late Eocene Ar (36.0–34.5 Ma) **Rock units** Waikato Coal Measures (Pukemiro Colliery) **Description** A simple oblong angiosperm leaf with smooth margin and strong midvein; the mostly alternate secondary veins depart at an acute to moderate angle from the midvein and curve slightly upwards as they approach the margin **Notes** Modern lauraceans are important economically and include avocados, bay laurels and cinnamon; common in tropical and subtropical regions, but extending to temperate parts of the world such as New Zealand; this specimen resembles *Cinnamomum* form and has two strong, opposite, basal secondary veins, characteristic of the Lauraceae generally. (1 cm)

'Pisonia' oliveri

Kingdom Plantae **Family** Nyctaginaceae? **Age** Late Eocene Ar (36.0–34.5 Ma) **Rock units** Waikato Coal Measures (Pukemiro Colliery) **Description** A large, simple angiosperm leaf with a toothed margin; small, rounded teeth; closely spaced secondary veins **Notes** Fossil leaves are often incomplete, such as this specimen, due to poor preservation, insect damage or damage during extraction; because fossil leaves are hidden in planes within sedimentary rocks, you usually need to split rocks with a hammer to find them; sometimes during this process your hammer has damaged a fossil, or the rock has broken part way through a leaf fossil. (5 cm)

Carcharius incurva

Phylum Vertebrata **Class** Chondrichthyes **Family** Carchariidae **Age** Early Eocene to Late Oligocene Dm?–Ld? (53–25 Ma?) **Rock units** Widespread in shallow-water formations **Description** Small, height to 20 mm, narrow, tapering to a sharp point, lightly recurved, with one weakly convex and one more strongly convex face, and smooth, sharp edges **Original material** Enamel, dentine **Habitat** Shallow offshore waters **Diet** Probably a predator of fishes **Notes** These narrow, lightly curved teeth are moderately common at some localities, particularly near 'Blind Jim's' in Te Whanga Lagoon, Chatham Island. (1 cm)

Flabellum circulare

Phylum Cnidaria **Class** Anthozoa **Subclass** Zoantharia **Order** Scleractinia **Family** Flabellidae **Age** Middle Eocene to Early Miocene Ab–Po (43–19 Ma) **Rock units** A wide variety of deep- to shallow-water formations **Description** Width 25–50 mm, almost circular in side view, but thin and flat and only slightly expanding outwards in the other plane; septae curving outwards at 180°–250° to produce a coin-shaped shell **Original material** Calcite **Habitat** Initially cemented to rocks, but old specimens became recurved to the point where they detached and lay on the seafloor **Diet** Filter-feeder **Notes** Specimens of this flat, almost circular coral usually occur in quite large numbers together on the one bedding plane, and many have the shell dissolved away, as in the photo. (1 cm)

Phylum Echinodermata **Class** Echinoidea **Order** Cidaroida **Family** Cidaridae **Age** Late Paleocene to Early Eocene Dt?–Dm (60–49.3 Ma) **Rock units** Red Bluff Tuff (Chatham Islands) **Description** Only the cylindrical spines are found; they are relatively large (20–35 mm long) and wide (up to 8 mm wide), bearing numerous rows of rounded knobs or spines, but the shape and sculpture are very variable **Original shell** High-magnesian calcite **Habitat** Shallow offshore soft sediments **Diet** Unknown; possibly seaweeds **Notes** These short, thick echinoid spines are abundant at the Chatham Islands, where they are found lying loose along the coast east of Tutuiri Stream, Tioriori, and around the shores of Lake Marakapia. (1 cm)

Arcopsis januaria

Phylum Mollusca **Class** Bivalvia **Family** Noetiidae **Age** Late Eocene to Early Oligocene Ak–Lwh (38.4–27.3 Ma) **Rock units** Waiareka and Deborah Volcanic Formations, Oamaru–Kakanui (Otago) **Description** Length 10–18 mm, strongly inflated, subrectangular with rounded ends; interior ventral margins smooth; many small, similar teeth along the entire hinge-line; sculpture different on the two valves, left valve with about 35 narrow, beaded radial riblets; right valve more finely sculptured, appearing almost smooth on many specimens **Original shell** Aragonite **Habitat** Burrowing shallowly in soft sediments **Diet** Filter-feeder **Notes** The only New Zealand member of this family of warm-water 'arc shells'. (5 mm)

Duplipecten waihaoensis

Phylum Mollusca **Class** Bivalvia **Family** Pectinidae **Age** Middle Eocene Ab (42.77–38.4 Ma) **Rock units** Waihao Greensand (S Canterbury) **Description** Height 60 mm, weakly inflated but quite thick-shelled; right valve exterior almost smooth, polished, but left valve with 12–14 prominent, smooth radial ribs; auricles separated from the disc by shallow grooves in the right valve but deep, undercut grooves in the left valve **Original shell** Calcite **Habitat** Lying free on the seabed in shallow water **Diet** Filter-feeder **Notes** A member of an evolutionary lineage of Eocene 'saucer scallops' that evolved a smooth shell which allowed them to swim well and avoid predatory fish. (1 cm)

'Serripecten' venosus

Phylum Mollusca **Class** Bivalvia **Family** Pectinidae **Age** Late Eocene to Early Oligocene Ak–Lwh (38.4–27.3 Ma) **Rock units** Widespread in shallow-water formations around Oamaru and in Westland **Description** Height 35–40 mm, thick-shelled, disc almost circular in shape; auricles prominent, almost square; right valve bearing 10–13 prominent, low, rounded, almost smooth radial ribs; left valve with many lower, narrower ribs, developing many scaly riblets; auricles with five to six fine, scaly radial riblets **Original shell** Calcite **Habitat** Byssally attached to hard objects **Diet** Filter-feeder **Notes** A member of a group of small scallops with few, prominent, rounded ribs, limited to Eocene–early Oligocene rocks. (1 cm)

Phylum Mollusca **Class** Bivalvia **Family** Ostreidae **Age** Middle Eocene Ab (42.77–38.4 Ma) **Rock units** Waihao Greensand (S Canterbury); shallow-water rocks in Northland, Westland and North Otago **Description** Small for the family (height 30–60 mm), shape highly variable, most specimens obliquely elongate; lower valve cupped, exterior sculptured with prominent, irregular radial ribs that form folds around the outer margin; right valve smooth, weakly convex; hinge area small; single adductor muscle scar crescentic **Original shell** Calcite **Habitat** Cemented to rocks in shallow water **Diet** Filter-feeder **Notes** A distinctive little ribbed oyster limited to Middle Eocene rocks. (1 cm)

Eucrassatella australis

Phylum Mollusca **Class** Bivalvia **Family** Crassatellidae **Age** Early to Late Eocene Dm–Ak (53.3–36.0 Ma) **Rock units** Common in shallow-water rocks throughout South Canterbury to North Otago **Description** Length 50–80 mm, thick, subtriangular in shape; exterior smooth except for a few commarginal ridges near the beak; hinge with prominent teeth; anterior and posterior adductor muscle scars small, similar in shape **Original shell** Aragonite **Habitat** Burrowing shallowly in soft sediments **Diet** Filter-feeder **Notes** This early member of the family is unusual in having weakly serrated interior ventral margins in some specimens. (1 cm)

Spirocolpus tophinus

Phylum Mollusca **Class** Gastropoda **Family** Turritellidae **Age** Middle Eocene to Late Oligocene Ab–Ld (42.77–25.2 Ma) **Rock units** Widespread in shallow-water formations in the South Island **Description** Height 25–35 mm, tall and narrowly conical, with at least 14 flat-sided whorls and a flat base; sculpture of two smooth, widely spaced spiral cords down the entire shell; outer lip with a deep, symmetrical sinus in the centre of the whorl **Original shell** Aragonite **Habitat** Shallowly buried in soft sediments **Diet** A ciliary deposit-feeder, gathering particles from the seafloor **Notes** An unusual small, simply sculptured, early turritellid; this family is very common and diverse in New Zealand. (1 cm)

Monalaria concinna

Phylum Mollusca **Class** Gastropoda **Family** Struthiolariidae **Age** Middle Eocene Ab (42.77–38.4 Ma) **Rock units** Common in shallow-water sandstone **Description** Height 30–40 mm, developing a strongly keeled shoulder on the last whorl; with large nodules around the keel; spiral sculpture of two prominent ridges on the last whorl; aperture strongly thickened, with smooth lips; outer lip with a deep sinus at the posterior end **Original shell** Aragonite **Habitat** Shallow sandy sediments, burrowing shallowly to feed **Diet** A ciliary deposit-feeder, gathering particles from the seafloor **Notes** Its thick, deeply sinuous outer lip and two prominent basal spiral cords are distinctive; limited to Middle Eocene rocks. (1 cm)

Phylum Mollusca **Class** Gastropoda **Family** Naticidae **Age** Middle to Late Eocene Ab–Ak (42.77–36.0 Ma) **Rock units** Waihao Greensand (S Canterbury), Hampden Formation (Otago) **Description** Height 15–20 mm, subspherical, width greater than height; smooth except for very fine spiral threads; last whorl enveloping most of the earlier shell; aperture large, D-shaped; widely open umbilicus bordered by a rounded, smooth ridge; inner lip callus thin except for a slight bulge in the centre of the umbilicus **Original shell** Aragonite **Habitat** Creeping, shallowly buried in sand **Diet** A carnivore of infaunal bivalves **Notes** Naticids leave characteristic bevelled, circular drill holes in bivalves. (1 cm)

Mauira biconica

Phylum Mollusca **Class** Gastropoda **Family** Volutidae **Age** Middle Eocene Ab (42.77–38.4 Ma) **Rock units** Waihao Greensand (S Canterbury), Hampden Formation (Otago) **Description** Height 80 mm, wide, with whorls angled low down, but riding up to the shoulder angle on the spire, producing a straight spire outline; low axial ridges on spire whorls are reduced to eight or nine prominent, sharp, curved nodules around the shoulder of the last whorl; with four folds on the columella; an obvious siphonal fasciole is margined by a sharp ridge **Original shell** Aragonite **Habitat** Shallow to deep sand, partially buried **Diet** Carnivore, a predator of bivalves **Notes** This large volute is limited to Middle Eocene rocks. (1 cm)

Athleta necopinata

Phylum Mollusca **Class** Gastropoda **Family** Volutidae **Age** Middle Eocene Ab (42.77–38.4 Ma) **Rock units** Waihao Greensand (S Canterbury and N Otago) **Description** Height 30–50 mm, with a low spire and a long last whorl; two rows of narrowly rounded nodules around the shoulder; exterior with flat-topped spiral cords; aperture long and narrow, with thickened lips; interior of outer lip with many fine ridges; inner lip spread widely over the lower surface of the shell; columella bearing five or six weak folds **Original shell** Aragonite **Habitat** Shallow sandy sediments, partially buried **Diet** Carnivore, a predator of bivalves **Notes** A member of a distinctive highly sculptured group of volutes limited to Eocene rocks. (1 cm)

Fascioplex liraecostata

Phylum Mollusca **Class** Gastropoda **Family** Melonginidae? **Age** Middle Eocene Ab (42.77–38.4 Ma) **Rock units** Waihao Greensand (S Canterbury) **Description** Height 25–35 mm, with a low spire and long, tapered last whorl; each whorl riding up onto the previous one to the peripheral keel; last whorl with a peripheral keel bearing triangular spines, and 3–5 similar keels below; entire exterior sculptured with fine, spiral ridges; columella with two narrow keels at the base; siphonal fasciole very prominent **Original shell** Aragonite **Habitat** Epifaunal on shallow sandy sediments **Diet** Presumably a predator of other molluscs **Notes** Another distinctively sculptured shell limited to Middle Eocene rocks. (1 cm)

Phylum Mollusca **Class** Gastropoda **Family** Speightiidae? **Age** Middle Eocene Ab (42.77–38.4 Ma) **Rock units** Waihao Greensand (S Canterbury), Hampden Formation (Otago) **Description** Height

50–90 mm, biconic, spire about half the total height; keel a short distance above the suture on the spire bearing 9–11 prominent, vertically compressed nodules per whorl; aperture with a shallow sinus in the upper part of the outer lip; anterior siphonal canal long, narrow, without a fasciole **Original shell** Aragonite **Habitat** Epifaunal on shallow to deep sand **Diet** Presumably a predator of worms and molluscs **Notes** This unusual shell is limited to Eocene rocks. (1 cm)

Superstes marshalli

Phylum Mollusca **Class** Gastropoda **Family** Ringiculidae **Age** Middle to Late Eocene Ab–Ak (42.77–36.0 Ma) **Rock units** Kapua Tuff (S Canterbury), Waihao Greensand (S Canterbury), Hampden Formation (Otago) **Description** Small (height 7–9 mm), almost spherical, with a low spire and an enveloping last whorl; sculpture of 20–27 pitted spiral grooves; aperture narrow, curved, with strongly thickened lips; interior of outer lip with two large nodules near base and 10 fine ridges above; inner lip with three prominent ridges near the base **Original shell** Aragonite **Habitat** Epifaunal on soft sediments **Diet** Foraminifera and copepod crustaceans **Notes** Large, subspherical ringiculids are widespread in Late Cretaceous to Eocene rocks. (5 mm)

Isis dactyla

Phylum Cnidaria **Class** Anthozoa **Subclass** Alcyonaria **Family** Isidae **Age** Early Oligocene to Early Miocene Lwh–Po (34.5–18.7 Ma) **Rock units** Widespread in limestone **Description** A coral composed of alternating flexible horny and rigid calcareous segments, of which only the calcareous segments are preserved; fossils are all short, almost cylindrical rods, mostly 20–40 mm long and up to 20 mm wide, with striated sides; the ends have a central sharp tip where they articulate with the horny segments

Original material Calcite **Habitat** Cemented to hard objects; all corals require an environment with no sediment **Diet** Filter-feeder **Notes** This 'hydrocoral' is the largest of several articulated genera and species in New Zealand Paleogene rocks. (1 cm)

Eupatagus rostratus zitteli

Phylum Echinodermata **Class** Echinoidea **Order** Spatangoida **Family** Spatangidae **Age** Early Oligocene to Early Miocene Lwh–Pl (34.5–15.9 Ma) **Rock units** Widespread in limestone **Description** Length 40–70 mm, oval, slightly longer than wide, with a weakly rounded dorsal surface and an almost flat ventral surface; anterior end with a shallow notch in the outline; five radial petals on the dorsal surface outlined by rows of small pores; areas of large, circular spine bases present on the dorsal surface between the petals **Original shell** High-magnesian calcite **Habitat** Shallow soft sediments **Diet** Unknown, possibly seaweeds **Notes** This relatively small, oval echinoid is distinguished by its shallow anterior notch. (1 cm)

Phylum Echinodermata **Class** Echinoidea **Order** Spatangoida **Family** Paleopneustidae **Age** Early Oligocene to Middle Miocene Lwh–Sw (34.5–11.01 Ma) **Rock units** Widespread in limestone **Description** Length 100–150 mm, almost smooth, low, subcircular, almost as wide as long, with a weakly convex dorsal surface and a flat ventral surface; a deep anterior groove on the dorsal surface extends into a deep anterior notch; five petals narrow, deeply impressed,

the anterior one lying in the anterior groove **Original shell** High-magnesian calcite **Habitat** Shallow soft sediments **Diet** Unknown; possibly seaweeds **Notes** This spectacular sea urchin is found in Oligocene limestone in New Zealand, particularly in Westland and around Oamaru; the deep anterior notch and groove are diagnostic. (5 cm)

Phylum Echinodermata **Class** Echinoidea **Order** Clypeasteroida **Family** Fibulariidae **Age** Early Oligocene to Early Miocene Lwh–Lw (34.5–21.7 Ma) **Rock units** Ototara Limestone (around Oamaru) **Description** Tiny (length 4–8 mm), evenly oval echinoids with little recognisable sculpture; dorsal surface with no holes; five petals very short, level with the shell surface, outlined by rows of pores; ventral surface with two holes **Original shell** High-magnesian calcite **Habitat** Shallow soft sediments **Diet** Unknown, possibly a deposit-feeder **Notes** Abundant in fine-grained, soft lime-

stone; occurs widely around the world in Eocene–Miocene rocks, and five species still live in the tropical Indo-West Pacific; therefore, it seems to indicate warm-water conditions. (1 cm)

Athlopecten athleta

Phylum Mollusca **Class** Bivalvia **Family** Pectinidae **Age** Late Oligocene Ld–Lw (27.3–21.7 Ma) **Rock units** Shallow-water limestone and sandstone throughout New Zealand **Description** Length 180–200 mm, thick, moderately inflated; exterior with 10–11 radial ribs and many secondary riblets on the left valve, about 20 more subdivided radial ribs on the right valve; crossed by thin, irregular commarginal lamellae on well-preserved shells; auricles large, separated from the disc by deep grooves **Original shell** Calcite **Habitat** Lying free on sandy sediments **Diet** Filter-feeder **Notes** The largest scallop known from New Zealand, very useful for identifying shallow-water late Oligocene rocks. (5 cm)

Lentipecten hochstetteri

Phylum Mollusca **Class** Bivalvia **Family** Pectinidae **Age** Late Oligocene Ld (27.3–25.2 Ma) **Rock units** Throughout New Zealand in sandstone and limestone **Description** Height 70–80 mm, length slightly greater than height, weakly inflated, smooth except for serrated dorsal margins to the auricles; auricles small, rounded, tapered towards the dorsal margin on the left valve **Original shell** Calcite **Habitat** Lying free on soft sediments, swimming to avoid predators **Diet** Filter-feeder **Notes** This species evolved from a weakly ribbed, earlier Ld species; it should not be confused with the more common Miocene species usually known by this name, which is taller than long. (1 cm)

Phylum Mollusca **Class** Bivalvia **Family** Cucullaeidae **Age** Late Oligocene Ld–Lw (27.3–21.7 Ma) **Rock units** Shallow-water limestone and sandstone throughout Canterbury and Otago **Description** Length 80–110 mm, thick-shelled, obliquely rectangular in shape, with exterior sculpture of very low, wide radial ribs, more prominent on the right valve than the left; many similar teeth across the whole hinge-line, directed vertically near the middle, but

longer and horizontal at each end; ventral margin crenulate **Original shell** Aragonite **Habitat** Partially buried in soft sediments **Diet** Filter-feeder **Notes** These large 'arc shells' lived throughout New Zealand until the end of Miocene time; Eocene species are smaller, and Miocene species are taller than *Cucullaea worthingtoni*. (1 cm)

Flemingostrea wollastoni

Phylum Mollusca **Class** Bivalvia **Family** Ostreidae **Age** Late Oligocene to Early Miocene Ld–Po (27.3–18.7 Ma) **Rock units** An abundant oyster throughout New Zealand **Description** Height 140–200 mm, up to 150 mm thick, oval; left (lower) valve shallowly cupped, right valve almost flat; exterior sculpture of growth ridges only; hinge a broad, prominent resilial area only; single adductor muscle scar crescentic, steeply inclined in the left valve, less so in the right valve **Original shell** Calcite **Habitat** Cemented together to form reefs in shallow water **Diet** Filter-feeder **Notes** These huge, thick oysters were abundant in New Zealand during the warm Oligocene and Miocene. (5 cm)

Spissatella subobesa

Phylum Mollusca **Class** Bivalvia **Family** Crassatellidae **Age** Late Oligocene Ld (27.3–25.2 Ma) **Rock units** Wharekuri Greensand (Waitaki Valley) **Description** Length 45–65 mm, long and low, with a short, rounded anterior end and a long, narrow, truncated posterior end; exterior closely and finely sculptured with narrow commarginal ridges, which weaken on the posterior end; hinge

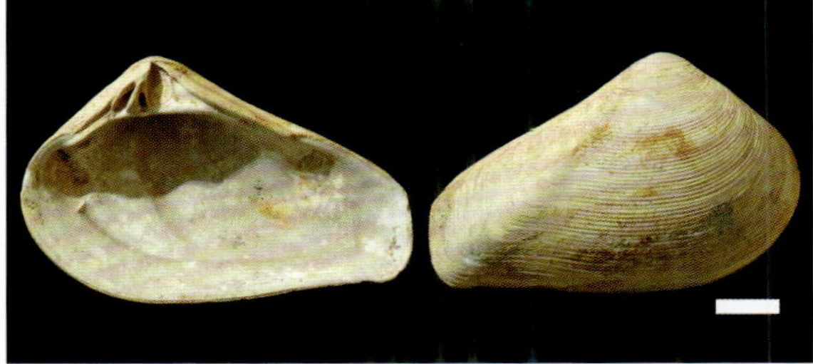

with prominent, narrow teeth and a large resilifer; ventral margin smooth **Original shell** Aragonite **Habitat** Burrowing shallowly in soft sediments **Diet** Filter-feeder **Notes** This genus of small, narrow, ribbed crassatellids is common in New Zealand shallow-water Oligocene and Miocene rocks. (1 cm)

Eucrassatella ampla

Phylum Mollusca **Class** Bivalvia **Family** Crassatellidae **Age** Late Oligocene to Late Miocene Ld–Tt (27.3–7.2 Ma) **Rock units** Shallow-water sandstone and mudstone throughout New Zealand **Description** Length 100–150 mm, very thick-shelled, smooth except for weak commarginal ridges near the beaks; anterior end evenly rounded, posterior with a flattened area extending from the beak to the posterior end; hinge very prominent, with thick, smooth teeth and a central resilifer; ventral margin smooth **Original**

shell Aragonite **Habitat** Burrowing shallowly in soft sediments **Diet** Filter-feeder **Notes** The largest New Zealand species of Crassatellidae, larger than *Eucrassatella australis* (see p. 70) and *E. marshalli* (Tk–Wp, 7.2–3.0 Ma), and more inflated and more weakly sculptured than *Spissatella* species (e.g. see above entry). (5 cm)

Phylum Mollusca **Class** Bivalvia **Family** Cardiidae **Age** Late Oligocene Ld (27.3–25.2 Ma) **Rock units** Sandstone in the Waikato, Waitaki Valley and Southland **Description** Height 60–70 mm, thin-shelled, strongly inflated, evenly rounded except that the posterior dorsal corner is sharply pointed in the right valve; sculpture of many narrow, prominent radial ribs; posterior area with lower and narrower ribs than the rest of the shell; hinge narrow, with small central teeth and small, widely separated anterior and posterior lateral teeth; ventral margin crenulate **Original shell** Aragonite **Habitat** Burrowing shallowly in soft sediments **Diet** Filter-feeder **Notes** A relatively small example of the diverse large cockles (Cardiidae) common in New Zealand Oligocene to Pliocene rocks. (1 cm)

Circomphalus speighti

Phylum Mollusca **Class** Bivalvia **Family** Veneridae **Age** Late Oligocene to Late Miocene Ld–Tt (27.3–7.2 Ma) **Rock units** Shallow-water rocks throughout New Zealand **Description** Length 40–60 mm, broadly oval, with two prominent, curved radial ribs, one posterior and one in the centre of the shell; sculpture of 10–12 high, thin commarginal lamellae, raised into weakly triangular spines where they cross the radial ribs; hinge with three narrow teeth in each valve; ventral margin finely crenulate **Original shell** Aragonite **Habitat** Burrowing shallowly off sandy ocean beaches **Diet** Filter-feeder **Notes** A long-ranging genus of 'frilled venus shells'; most younger species lack the central radial rib. (1 cm)

Guildfordia sp.

Phylum Mollusca **Class** Gastropoda **Family** Turbinidae **Age** Late Oligocene Ld–Lw (27.3–21.7 Ma) **Rock units** Otekaike Limestone (N Otago and S Canterbury) **Description** Width 50–60 mm (not including spines), low and wide, with a row of 10 long, narrow, forward-directed spines around the outer edge; centre of the base smooth, with an obvious central hollow; the rest of the surface sculptured with many small nodules **Original shell** Aragonite **Habitat**

Epifaunal on shallow offshore soft sediments **Diet** Unknown; a deposit-feeder, or grazed sponges or bryozoans **Notes** A tropical Pacific genus; one of many indications of warm conditions in New Zealand during Oligocene and Miocene time. (1 cm)

Xenophora prognata

Phylum Mollusca **Class** Gastropoda **Family** Xenophoridae **Age** Late Oligocene to Middle Miocene Ld–Sl (27.3–12.98 Ma) **Rock units** Shallow-water sandstone and mudstone throughout New Zealand **Description** Width 80–150 mm, low-conical; outer edge of the upper surface protruding as a rim around the base; large stones and empty bivalve shells up to 50 mm across are cemented to the lower rim of each whorl; upper surface sculptured with wavy axial ridges and spiral cords; base flat, weakly sculptured, with-

out an umbilicus **Original shell** Aragonite **Habitat** Epifaunal on offshore soft sediments **Diet** A deposit-feeder, gathering particles from the seafloor **Notes** A 'carrier shell', camouflaging its shell with stones and empty shells cemented to the outside. (5 cm)

Phylum Mollusca **Class** Gastropoda **Family** Turritellidae **Age** Late Oligocene Ld (27.3–25.2 Ma) **Rock units** Chatton Formation (Southland), Wharekuri Greensand (Waitaki Valley) **Description** Height 110–155 mm, tall and narrowly conical; early whorls flat-sided, later one weakly concave; base almost flat; sculpture of a low spiral swelling around the top of each whorl and two narrow spiral cords around the lower part; outer lip thin, with a wide, moderately deep sinus near the centre of the lip **Original shell** Aragonite **Habitat** Shallowly buried in soft sediments **Diet** A ciliary filter-feeder, gathering particles from the seafloor **Notes** These huge turritellids are common in New Zealand Oligocene and Miocene rocks. (5 cm)

Cirsotrema lyratum

Phylum Mollusca **Class** Gastropoda **Family** Epitoniidae **Age** Early Oligocene to Early Miocene Lwh–Pl (34.5–15.9 Ma) **Rock units** Shallow-water greensand and limestone throughout New Zealand **Description** Height 50–90 mm, tall and narrow, with 10–12 strongly inflated whorls; sculpture of 13–15 prominent, thick axial ridges per whorl; crossed by several spiral ridges and many fine spiral threads; aperture circular, with thick lips; base encircled by an obvious spiral ridge **Original shell** Calcite **Habitat** Epifaunal in shallow water **Diet** A carnivore grazing on corals and sea anemones **Notes** This group of beautifully sculptured 'wentle-trap' shells is common in New Zealand. (1 cm)

Magnatica planispira

Phylum Mollusca **Class** Gastropoda **Family** Naticidae **Age** Early Oligocene to Early Miocene Ld–Pl (27.3–15.9 Ma) **Rock units** Shallow-water formations throughout New Zealand **Description** Height 40–65 mm, almost spherical, robust and thick-shelled; exterior smooth; aperture large, D-shaped, with a thickened inner lip; umbilicus narrow but deep **Original shell** Aragonite **Habitat** Creeping, shallowly buried in sand **Diet** A carnivore of infaunal bivalves, drilling through their shells with a special boring organ **Notes** Some specimens of this large 'moon snail' are found with the flat, smooth aragonite operculum in place in the aperture; this gastropod leaves characteristic large, bevelled drill-holes in bivalves. (1 cm)

Parasyrinx subalta

Phylum Mollusca **Class** Gastropoda **Family** Cochlespiridae **Age** Late Oligocene Ld–Lw (27.3–21.7 Ma) **Rock units** Wharekuri Formation (Waitaki Valley), Otekaike Limestone and Mount Harris Formation (Otago and Canterbury) **Description** Height 17–32 mm, tall and narrow, with a long siphonal canal; whorls sharply keeled at the centre; sutural ramp steep, slightly concave; upper part of the sutural ramp smooth, remainder of the surface sculptured with fine spiral threads; outer lip with a deep U-shaped sinus with its apex near the centre of the sutural ramp **Original shell**

Aragonite **Habitat** Epifaunal on offshore soft sediments **Diet** A carnivore of worms and molluscs **Notes** Highly diverse cochlespirids are common in New Zealand Oligocene–Miocene rocks. (1 cm)

Phylum Mollusca **Class** Gastropoda **Family** Pseudotomidae **Age** Late Oligocene Ld (27.3–25.2 ma) **Rock Units** Chatton Formation, Southland **Description** Height 30–50 mm, with a deeply concave sutural ramp; last whorl gradually tapered to a short, wide anterior canal, forming a low fasciole; sculpture of many prominent, narrow, widely spaced spiral cords; posterior sinus shallow, occupying the sutural ramp. **Original shell** Aragonite **Habitat** Epifaunal on shallow soft sediments **Diet** A carnivore of worms and molluscs **Notes** An example of a very diverse genus common throughout New Zealand Eocene to Pliocene rocks. (1 cm)

Fissidentalium solidum

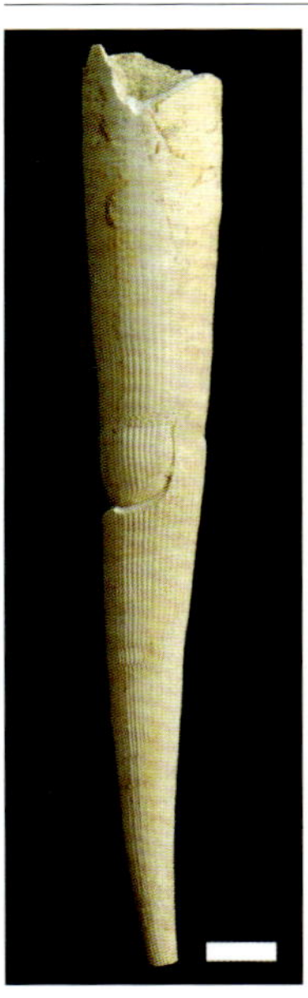

Phylum Mollusca **Class** Scaphopoda **Family** Dentaliidae **Age** Late Oligocene to Late Miocene Ld–Tt (27.3–7.2 Ma) **Rock units** Common in shallow-water formations **Description** Length 100–150 mm, thick, tubular, open at both ends; obviously curved near the narrow end, but almost straight for most of its length, sculptured with about 45 low, rounded, closely spaced longitudinal ribs; narrow aperture with a long, narrow slit **Original shell** Aragonite **Habitat** Partially buried in soft sediments, with the narrow end protruding **Diet** A selective carnivore of foraminifera **Notes** Large 'tusk shells' are common in many New Zealand rocks, although the time ranges of most species are poorly understood. (1 cm)

'Cocos' zeylandica

Kingdom Plantae **Family** Arecaceae **Age** Late Oligocene to Late Miocene Ld–Tk (27.3–5.33 Ma) **Rock units** Mangonui Formation (Coopers Beach, Mangonui), Waikiekie Quarry (Northland), near Matawai (eastern North Island) **Description** Preserved as flattened oval nuts, width 30–40 mm, with longitudinal shallow striations/grooves on the surface and three distinctive small apertures at one end **Notes** Although these have long been referred to as New Zealand fossil coconuts, they may not belong to the *Cocos* genus, hence the inverted commas; a closer resemblance to the South American palm genus *Parajubaea* has been suggested. (1 cm)

Nothofagus oliveri

Kingdom Plantae **Family** Nothofagaceae **Age** Middle to Late Miocene Sw–Tt (12.98–7.2 Ma) **Rock units** Longford Formation (Nuggety Creek, Murchison) **Description** Simple, broad angiosperm leaf, surface up to 170 mm long and 60 mm wide, with obtuse to acute apex, base probably wedge-shaped, and serrate margin; the midvein is straight, and the secondary veins are regularly spaced and strong and curve slightly upwards near the margin **Notes** *Nothofagus* ('southern beech') species have been a significant part of the New Zealand flora since the Late Cretaceous; the leaves of this fossil are considerably larger than those from any of the species of *Nothofagus* growing in New Zealand today. (1 cm)

Phylum Chordata **Class** Chondrichthyes **Family** Lamnidae **Age** Early Oligocene to Pliocene Lwh–Wp? (34.5–3.0 Ma) **Rock units**

Widespread in limestone **Description** Height of enamel to 120 mm, width of enamel to 117 mm, symmetrical and widely triangular, with one flat face and one convex face; edges finely serrated; the root, attached to most specimens, is wide, low and gently curved **Original material** Enamel, dentine **Habitat** Offshore mid-waters **Diet** Probably a predator of whales **Notes** This extinct 'super great white' shark had the largest known shark teeth, and must have been a fearsome predator up to 20 m long; these huge teeth occur rarely in New Zealand Oligocene to Pliocene rocks. (5 cm)

Isurus retroflexus

Phylum Chordata **Class** Chondrichthyes **Family** Lamnidae **Age** Late Oligocene to Early Miocene Ld–Pl (27.3–15.9 Ma) **Rock units** Widespread but uncommon **Description** Height 25–30 mm, shaped much like *Carcharodon* species (see above entry); that is, relatively wide and with one flat and one convex face, but

inclined strongly inwards towards the inside of the mouth, and with smooth edges **Original material** Enamel, dentine **Habitat** Offshore mid-waters **Diet** Probably a predator of fishes **Notes** The shape is distinctive, with its lateral curve towards the interior of the mouth. (1 cm)

Cetacea indet.

Phylum Chordata **Class** Mammalia **Order** Cetacea **Age** Late Miocene Tt (11–7.2 Ma) **Rock units** Palliser Group (Wairarapa Coast) **Description** Small to large object with regular or irregular outline, often sharply defined against the matrix of the enclosing rock; internal sponge-like structure characteristic of bone which can vary in density; may have round holes of varying sizes (nerve and blood vessel conduits, or due to predation); colour often pale, white-grey or cream and often a shade of brown **Original material** Calcium phosphate **Habitat** Open marine; fossils can occur in any marine sedimentary rock **Diet** Whales are carnivorous; baleen whales are filter-feeders (plankton and crustaceans); toothed whales eat anything (mainly fish and squid) **Notes** Fragmentary whale bone fossils are relatively common in marine sediments of Eocene to Recent age in New Zealand; they preserve well because they are large and lumpy; sometimes it is difficult to distinguish fossil bone from fossil wood; the larger open holes in this bone have been formed by recent rock-boring clams and are not part of the original fossil. (5 cm, 1 cm)

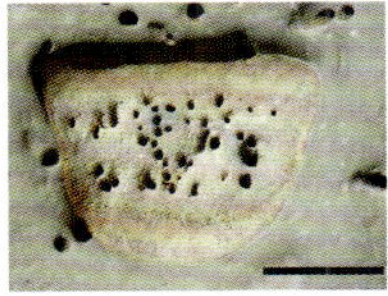

Platyhelia distans

Phylum Cnidaria **Class** Anthozoa **Subclass** Zoantharia **Order** Scleractinia **Family** Rhizangiidae **Age** Miocene Pl–Tk (18.7–5.33 Ma) **Rock units** Widespread in shallow-water formations **Description** Fragments up to 100 mm across and 20–50 mm thick of an originally encrusting, colonial coral with closely spaced coralites each 3–9 mm in width; when closely spaced the coralites form quadrangular to hexagonal shapes, but when separated by the 1–4 mm-thick outer layer they are circular **Original material** Calcite **Habitat** A colonial, reef-forming coral cemented to hard objects in shallow water **Diet** Filter-feeder **Notes** This is one of few reef-forming corals found throughout New Zealand shallow-water Miocene rocks, as far south as Oamaru. (1 cm)

Bathylasma aucklandicum

Phylum Arthropoda **Class** Crustacea **Family** Pachylasmidae **Age** Late Oligocene to Pliocene Ld–Wp (27.3–3.0 Ma) **Rock units** Widespread in offshore limestone and sandstone **Description** Height up to 180 mm, almost cylindrical, with six tall, thin, narrow plates sculptured with obvious delicate, transverse growth ridges; the plates covering the aperture are thick and triangular, with weak radial ridges on the outside **Original shell** Calcite **Habitat** Cemented to hard objects in deep water **Diet** Filter-feeder **Notes** This species is unusual for deep-water 'barnacles' from New Zealand because some specimens are almost complete shells; the illustrated specimen has curved around during growth. (1 cm)

Austromegabalanus miodecorus

Phylum Arthropoda **Class** Crustacea **Family** Balanidae **Age** Middle Miocene to Late Pliocene Sw–Wm (13–2.4 Ma) **Rock units** Common in many shallow-water rocks **Description** Height up to 50 mm, thick-shelled, with weakly inflated sides tapering to the aperture;

six main shell plates almost smooth, with wide, white outer surfaces and narrow, pink depressed areas between them; plates closing the aperture are narrowly triangular, thick, the smaller two each with a narrow, protruding ridge **Original shell** Calcite **Habitat** Cemented to hard objects in shallow water **Diet** Filter-feeder **Notes** A typical 'acorn barnacle', living in shallow water attached to molluscan shells, rather than coating rocks in the intertidal zone. (1 cm)

Leptomithrax sp.

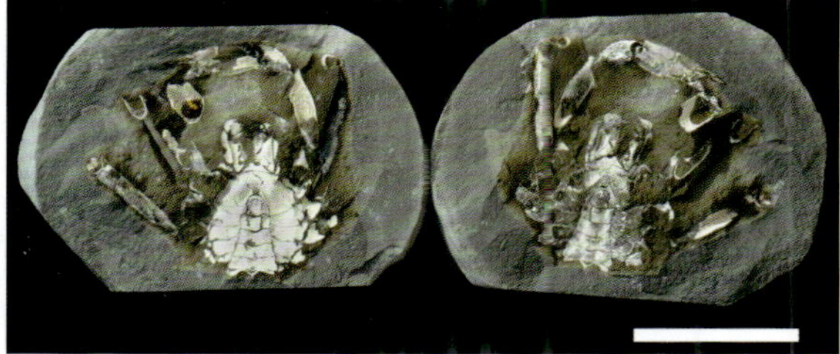

Phylum Arthropoda **Class** Crustacea **Family** Majidae **Age** Late Miocene to Early Pliocene Tt–Wo (11–3.6 Ma) **Rock units** Matemateaonga Formation (central North Island) **Description** Carapace 40–50 mm wide, subcircular, with 8–10 large spines around the outline; small eye sockets and two large mouthparts visible at the front; underside of the (female) carapace has a long abdomen with six segments; the pincers and the legs are long and narrow, the pincer-bearing legs with longitudinal ridges and fine pustules on the surface **Original shell** Calcium phosphate **Habitat** Offshore soft sediments **Diet** Scavenger **Notes** members of the 'spider crab' family, with long, narrow legs and a spiny carapace, live in the subtidal zone and offshore. (5 cm)

Tumidocarcinus giganteus

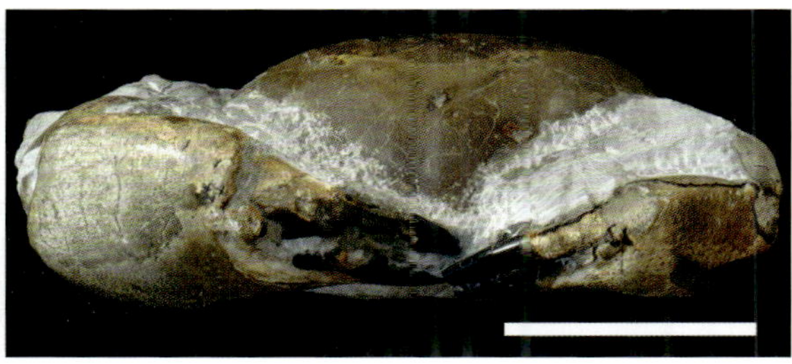

Phylum Arthropoda **Class** Crustacea **Family** Xanthidae **Age** Middle to Late Miocene Sl–Tt (15.1–7.2 Ma) **Rock units** Widespread in concretions in offshore mudstone **Description** Very large (carapace up to 150 mm wide), subcircular, almost smooth, evenly rounded, with weak furrows across the carapace; the right pincer is extremely large and wide, up to 180 mm long; the left pincer is a little smaller **Original shell** Calcium phosphate **Habitat** Offshore soft sediments **Diet** Scavenger **Notes** This enormous, smoothly rounded species is the most common New Zealand fossil crab; the right pincer of males grows relatively larger as the animal grows (allometric growth) and retains its original black colour on many fossils. (5 cm)

Pachymagas forbesi

Phylum Brachiopoda **Family** Terebratellidae **Age** Early Miocene Pl (18.7–15.9 Ma) **Rock units** '*Pachymagas* bed' in Otahu Formation (Clifden, Southland) **Description** Length 40–50 mm, evenly oval, vertically compressed; pedicle foramen small; smooth apart from a shallow sulcus in the upper valve, matched by a fold in the lower (pedicle) valve and an obvious flexure in the posterior margins **Original shell** Calcite **Habitat** The small pedicle foramen suggests *Pachymagas* probably lived like *Neothyris* (see p. 105), lying on the seabed and rolling in currents **Diet** Filter-feeder **Notes** This large group of smooth brachiopods with a shallow sulcus in

the shell is common in limestone and shallow-water shellbeds throughout the Middle Cenozoic. (1 cm)

Rhizothyris trigonalis

Phylum Brachiopoda **Family** Terebratellidae **Age** Early Miocene Pl (18.7–15.9 Ma) **Rock units** Forest Hill Limestone (Southland), limestone in Canterbury **Description** Length 30–40 mm, wide and

very compressed, with an unusually straight anterior margin, weakly rectangular outlines, a very short beak and a very small pedicle foramen; smooth except for a very shallow, variable sulcus flexing the posterior valve margin **Original shell** Calcite **Habitat** The very small pedicle foramen suggest that *Rhizothyris*

lived loose on the seabed **Diet** Filter-feeder **Notes** The shape, strongly compressed vertically and weakly rectangular in outline, makes this an unusual brachiopod in the New Zealand fauna. (1 cm)

Erihadrosia epsilon

Phylum Brachiopoda **Family** Terebratellidae **Age** Miocene Pl–Sw (18.7–11 Ma) **Rock units** Weka Pass area (N Canterbury), Clifden section (Southland) **Description** Height 70–80 mm, very elongate, strongly inflated dorsoventrally, with a thick shell, a very small, strongly hooked beak and an extremely small pedicle foramen; smooth apart from a very weak flexure in the posterior valve margins **Original shell** Calcite **Habitat** The very small pedicle foramen suggests that *Erihadrosia* lay loose on the seabed **Diet** Filter-feeder **Notes** *Erihadrosia* is very unusual in having a vertically inflated shape, a tall height–width ratio, and almost straight, parallel left and right margins. (5 cm)

Limopsis zitteli

Phylum Mollusca **Class** Bivalvia **Family** Limopsidae **Age** Early Oligocene to Middle Miocene Lwh–Sw (34.5–11 Ma) **Rock units** Common in shallow-water sandstone and mudstone **Description** Height 30–45 mm, thick-shelled, weakly inflated, weakly sculptured; slightly elongate towards the posterior; ventral margin with a flat, smooth bevelled edge; hinge with many similar, weakly curved teeth, long at the ends but reduced in height in the centre by the downward growth of the wide, triangular ligamental pit beneath the beak **Original shell** Aragonite **Habitat** Burrowing shallowly in soft sediments **Diet** Filter-feeder **Notes** The largest species in a large group of small bivalves found throughout Late Cretaceous to Pliocene rocks. (1 cm)

Phylum Mollusca **Class** Bivalvia **Family** Glycymerididae **Age** Middle Miocene to Early Pliocene Sc–Wo (15.9–3.6 Ma) **Rock units** Shallow-water formations in the eastern North Island, Marlborough and Westland **Description** Height 85–115 mm, thick-shelled, higher than long, weakly triangular in shape; sculptured with many fine radial grooves; ligamental area wide, with up to 10 grooves; hinge with many similar, curved teeth on each side, obliterated in the centre by downwards growth of the ligamental area; ventral margin coarsely crenulate **Original shell** Aragonite **Habitat** Burrowing shallowly in soft sediments **Diet** Filter-feeder **Notes** The largest New Zealand glycymeridid; distinguished from *Cucullaea* (see p. 78) by its taller shape, shorter hinge with differently shaped teeth, and weaker sculpture. (5 cm)

Serripecten yahliensis

Phylum Mollusca **Class** Bivalvia **Family** Pectinidae **Age** Miocene Po–Tt (21.7–7.2 Ma) **Rock units** Shallow-water sandstone (Po–Sw), Patutahi Limestone (Gisborne, Tt) **Description** Length 100–160 mm, longer than high; left valve weakly inflated, right valve strongly inflated; sculpture of right valve of 40–50 narrow, widely spaced radial ribs, coarsely serrated on their outer edges; left valve with 100–120 narrow, closely spaced, finely serrated radial ribs; auricles very wide, separated from the disc by deep grooves; byssal notch small in adults **Original shell** Calcite **Habitat** Lying free on soft sediments **Diet** Filter-feeder **Notes** The last in a long line of finely serrated scallops that increased in size through Eocene–Miocene time. (5 cm)

Sectipecten wollastoni

Phylum Mollusca **Class** Bivalvia **Family** Pectinidae **Age** Late Miocene to Early Pleistocene Tt–Wn (11–1.6 Ma) **Rock units** Shallow-water formations, Momoe-a-Toa Shellbed (Chatham Island) **Description** Height 95–110 mm, subcircular, moderately and evenly inflated; auricles almost square; sculpture very prominent, of six to seven high, flat-topped, sharp-edged radial folds on each valve, and many narrower radial ribs and grooves, becoming more subdivided down the shell; folds wider on the right valve, interlocking with narrower ones on the left valve **Original shell** Calcite **Habitat** Lying free on soft sediments **Diet** Filter-feeder **Notes** Part of a gradually evolving species; common in late Miocene rocks (11–5.3 Ma), but afterwards increasingly rare and limited to very shallow water. (5 cm)

Lima colorata

Phylum Mollusca **Class** Bivalvia **Family** Limidae **Age** Miocene Po–Tt (21.7–7.2 Ma) **Rock units** Shallow offshore sandstone **Description** Height 65–110 mm, asymmetrical, anterior margin markedly longer than the posterior one; posterior auricle large, thick, but anterior one very small; sculptured with 18–23 prominent radial ribs of almost square cross-section, bearing sparse spines, and crenulating the ventral margin; anterior margin with a shallow byssal gape below the auricle; ligamental area wide, triangular, with a large central ligamental pit **Original shell** Calcite **Habitat** Byssally attached to hard objects **Diet** Filter-feeder **Notes** Many specimens of this unusually large species of *Lima* retain their red colour. (1 cm)

Phylum Mollusca **Class** Bivalvia **Family** Anomiidae **Age** Latest Oligocene to Early Miocene Lw–Pl (25.2–15.9 Ma) **Rock units** Mount Harris Formation (Oamaru) **Description** Height 35–55 mm, both valves thick; sculptured with many narrow, spiny radial riblets; cemented by a calcified, pale brown byssal plug passing through a hole in the right valve; interior with a single circular muscle scar in the right valve, and two circular scars in the left valve; hinge with a triangular ligamental 'tooth' in the right valve and a matching depression in the left valve **Original shell** Calcite **Habitat** Cemented to other shells **Diet** Filter-feeder **Notes** Species of *Pododesmus* are found mainly in tropical American waters at present, another indicator of warm conditions. (1 cm)

Glyptoactis (Fasciculicardia) subintermedia

Phylum Mollusca **Class** Bivalvia **Family** Carditidae **Age** Miocene Po–Sl (21.7–13 Ma) **Rock units** Shallow-water sandstone in Northland and Southland **Description** Length 50–70 mm, thick-shelled, strongly inflated, with prominent sculpture of 28–30 narrow radial ribs, each interspace wider than one rib, bearing small nodules on rib crests; hinge wide, bearing two narrow teeth and a wide socket in the left valve and a very wide central tooth and narrow sockets in the right valve; ventral margin coarsely crenulate **Original shell** Aragonite **Habitat** Burrowing shallowly in soft sediments **Diet** Filter-feeder **Notes** This species preferred warm water; not found in the cooler-water Miocene faunas of Canterbury and North Otago. (5 cm)

Nemocardium patulum

Phylum Mollusca **Class** Bivalvia **Family** Cardiidae **Age** Latest Oligocene to Late Miocene Lw–Sw (2.25–11 Ma) **Rock units** Shallow offshore sandstone and mudstone **Description** Height 65–95 mm, thick-shelled, strongly inflated, somewhat rectangular in shape; sculptured with many fine, closely spaced radial riblets, coarser over the sharply defined posterior area than elsewhere; riblets on the posterior area bear small, sharp nodules; hinge with large, obvious central hinge teeth and widely separated anterior and posterior lateral teeth; ventral margin crenulate **Original shell** Aragonite **Habitat** Burrowing shallowly in soft sediments **Diet** Filter-feeder **Notes** A spectacular 'cockle' resembling, but even larger than, the living tropical Pacific species *Nemocardium bechei*. (5 cm)

Atamarcia thomsoni

Phylum Mollusca **Class** Bivalvia **Family** Veneridae **Age** Middle to Late Miocene Sl–Tt (15.1–7.2 Ma) **Rock units** Shallow-water formations in the Gisborne district, South Wairarapa and Westland **Description** Height 60–70 mm, subtriangular, with strongly inflated beaks but almost flat sides; beaks curved strongly forwards; sculpture of many shallow, narrow, widely spaced, commarginal grooves, central area smooth and polished; hinge with three narrow teeth and sockets in each valve; ventral margin smooth **Original shell** Aragonite **Habitat** Burrowing in soft sediments **Diet** Filter-feeder **Notes** Common on the Palliser Bay coast; most specimens are closed, articulated shells. (1 cm)

Phylum Mollusca **Class** Bivalvia **Family** Veneridae **Age** Middle to Late Miocene Sw–Tt (13–7.2 Ma) **Rock units** Shallow-water formations **Description** Height 42–50 mm, circular, thick-shelled, weakly inflated; sculpture of many narrow, widely spaced commarginal lamellae; lunule depressed, defined by a bounding ridge; hinge with three teeth and sockets in each valve **Original shell** Aragonite **Habitat** Burrowing shallowly off sandy ocean beaches **Diet** Filter-feeder **Notes** The subgenus *Dosinia (Kereia)* is defined by its near-circular shape and prominent commarginal lamellae; the Late Miocene (Tk, 7 Ma) to living species *Dosinia (Kereia) greyi* differs in its greater inflation and more rounded posterior outline. (1 cm)

Struthiolaria calcar

Phylum Mollusca **Class** Gastropoda **Family** Struthiolariidae **Age** Latest Oligocene to Middle Miocene Lw–Sw (25.2–11 Ma) **Rock units** Common in shallow-water rocks **Description** Height 25–55 mm, with a stepped spire and a rounded last whorl; shoulder sharply angled at about two-thirds of whorl height, bearing sharp nodules around the angle; lower angulation on last whorl with smaller nodules; other sculpture of many fine spiral ribs; aperture oval, with a pointed anterior end; lips strongly thickened **Original shell** Aragonite **Habitat** Shallow sandy sediments, burrowing shallowly to feed **Diet** A ciliary deposit-feeder, gathering particles from the seafloor **Notes** A long-ranging species, followed in the late Miocene–Pliocene by a radiation of several species. (1 cm)

Struthiolaria (Callusaria) callosa

Phylum Mollusca **Class** Gastropoda **Family** Struthiolariidae **Age** Middle to Late Miocene Sl–Tt (15.1–7.2 Ma) **Rock units** Many shallow-water formations **Description** Height 40–70 mm, short and wide; smooth apart from prominent, sharp nodules around the shoulder angulation and smaller ones around the lower angulation on the last whorl; aperture smooth, strongly thickened, with a wide, sinuous outer lip and a hugely developed callus covering the underside of the last whorl **Original shell** Aragonite **Habitat** Shallow sandy sediments, burrowing shallowly to feed **Diet** A ciliary deposit-feeder, gathering particles from the seafloor **Notes** This very distinctive shell is a useful index fossil of Sl–Tt age. (1 cm)

Maoricrypta radiata

Phylum Mollusca **Class** Gastropoda **Family** Calyptraeidae **Age** Middle Miocene to Early Pliocene Sw–Wo (13–3.6 Ma) **Rock units** Many shallow-water formations **Description** Length 40–90 mm, canoe-shaped, with a slightly curled apex and an internal septum; a single muscle scar on the right side of the septum; sculpture variable, from completely smooth to strong longitudinal ribs, all forms living in the same piles of specimens **Original shell** Aragonite **Habitat** Sedentary, attached to shells and rocks, and piled up attached to each other **Diet** Filter-feeder **Notes** This is the only species of the New Zealand genus *Maoricrypta* that forms tall piles of specimens. (1 cm)

Phylum Mollusca **Class** Gastropoda **Family** Naticidae **Age** Early to Middle Miocene Pl–Sw (18.7–11 Ma) **Rock units** Abundant in shallow-water rocks **Description** Height 30–65 mm, subspherical, smooth, with a low spire, almost enveloped by the last whorl; last whorl with a slightly flattened outline; aperture D-shaped;

inner lip callus hugely thickened, almost completely filling the umbilicus **Original shell** Aragonite **Habitat** Creeping, shallowly buried in soft sediments **Diet** Drills through the shells of infaunal bivalves with a special boring organ **Notes** Although one species still lives in the northern North Island, almost all *Polinices* species are tropical sand-flat burrowers, leaving circular, bevelled drill-holes in bivalve shells as a record of their predatory habit. (1 cm)

Echinophoria pollens

Phylum Mollusca **Class** Gastropoda **Family** Cassidae **Age** Early to Middle Miocene Po–Sc (21.7–15.1 Ma) **Rock units** Shallow-water sandstone **Description** Height 45–70 mm, subspherical, with a short spire, mostly enveloped by the last whorl; sculpture of three to five rows of large, pointed nodules on the last whorl, the uppermost also present on the spire; nodules variable in size and spacing, 7–12 per whorl; aperture large, oval, with strongly thickened lips **Original shell** Aragonite **Habitat** Epifaunal on soft substrates **Diet** A carnivore, mostly a predator of sea urchins **Notes** This is the most strongly sculptured species of New Zealand Cassidae, and a member of a warm-water genus. (1 cm)

Austrofusus coerulescens

Phylum Mollusca **Class** Gastropoda **Family** Buccinulidae **Age** Late Miocene Tk (7.2–5.3 Ma) **Rock units** Common in shallow-water rocks **Description** Height 20–50 mm, narrow for the genus; whorls evenly and strongly convex apart from the concave sutural ramp; sculpture of rows of small, rounded nodules, three or four rows on spire whorls and six to seven on the last whorl, and rounded spiral ribs on the base; siphonal canal rather short, strongly twisted, with weakly defined fasciole **Original shell** Aragonite **Habitat** Epifaunal on soft substrates **Diet** A generalised carnivore **Notes** This small, distinctively sculptured species is an index fossil of Kapitean time throughout New Zealand. (1 cm)

Austrofusus magnificus

Phylum Mollusca **Class** Gastropoda **Family** Buccinulidae **Age** Early to Middle Miocene Pl–Sl (18.7–13 Ma) **Rock units** Clifden section, Waiau River (Southland) **Description** Height 45–60 mm, with moderately tall spire and moderately long, twisted anterior canal; predominant sculpture of two rows of large, vertically compressed, sharp nodules, the upper forming the lower edge of a concave sutural ramp; remainder of surface bearing many fine spiral ridges, more prominent on the base **Original shell** Aragonite **Habitat** Epifaunal on shallow-water soft sediments **Diet** A generalised carnivore **Notes** The most strongly sculptured of many *Austrofusus* species occurring throughout New Zealand Cenozoic rocks. (1 cm)

Phylum Mollusca **Class** Gastropoda **Family** Buccinulidae **Age** Middle to Late Miocene Sl–Tt (15.1–7.2 Ma) **Rock units** Common in shallow-water formations **Description** Height 28–35 mm, short and wide, with a prominently 'rolled' shoulder produced by a shallow spiral sulcus around the last whorl; sculpture weak apart from five to six low, rounded spiral ribs around the base of the last whorl; siphonal fasciole very prominent, short and wide, bordered by a sharp spiral rib **Original shell** Aragonite **Habitat** Epifaunal on soft sediments **Diet** A scavenger **Notes** Similar to *Cominella adspersa* (living) but much smaller; some specimens retain the original colour pattern of speckled markings on the spiral ribs. (1 cm)

Penion crawfordi

Phylum Mollusca **Class** Gastropoda **Family** Buccinulidae **Age** Middle to Late Miocene Sl–Tt (15.1–7.2 Ma) **Rock units** Many shallow-water formations **Description** Height 100–120 mm, with a low spire, a prominent shoulder angulation and a deeply concave sutural ramp; sculpture of low spiral ribs, prominent around the centre of the last whorl and on the base, and small to long, narrow, vertically compressed nodules around the shoulder angle, and one or two rows of lower nodules around the lower angulation; siphonal canal long, curved, with a prominent siphonal fasciole **Original shell** Aragonite **Habitat** Epifaunal on soft sediments **Diet** A generalised carnivore **Notes** The most diverse genus of large 'whelks' in shallow-water faunas. (5 cm)

Spinomelon parki

Phylum Mollusca **Class** Gastropoda **Family** Volutidae **Age** Early Miocene Po–Pl (21.7–15.9 Ma) **Rock units** Mount Harris Formation (South Canterbury and North Otago) **Description** Height 100–135 mm, spire conical, a third of the total height; protoconch with a sharp spike on the apex; sculpture of 12–15 narrow axial ribs per whorl, forming nodules at the shoulder angulation; last whorl narrow and almost parallel-sided; aperture with lightly thickened lips; columella with five prominent folds **Original shell** Aragonite **Habitat** Shallow-water sand and mud, partially buried **Diet** Carnivore predating bivalves **Notes** The genus *Spinomelon* (Eocene to present) was probably ancestral to the more diverse New Zealand genus *Alcithoe*. (5 cm)

Comitas fusiformis

Phylum Mollusca **Class** Gastropoda **Family** Pseudomelatomidae **Age** Late Oligocene to Early Miocene Ld–Pl (27.3–15.9 Ma)

Rock units Widespread in shallow-water formations **Description** Height 30–60 mm, tall and narrow; whorls weakly shouldered, with a concave sutural ramp; sculpture of low, rounded, curved axial ribs commencing at the edge of the ramp, 10–13 per whorl; crossed by low spiral ridges; siphonal canal almost straight; outer lip with a narrowly U-shaped sinus with its apex slightly above the centre of the sutural ramp **Original shell** Aragonite **Habitat** Epifaunal on soft sediments **Diet** A carnivore of molluscs and worms **Notes** Type species of a widespread genus, highly diverse offshore in tropical seas. (1 cm)

Phylum Mollusca **Class** Gastropoda **Family** Borsoniidae **Age** Early Miocene Po–Pl (21.7–15.9 Ma) **Rock Units** Pakaurangi Formation, Northland **Description** Height 40–60 mm, strongly biconic, spire outline almost straight; sutural ramp weakly concave, with a row of large, narrow nodules around the shoulder angle; about 12 prominent spiral cords around the base; posterior sinus narrow, its apex at the peripheral nodule row **Original shell** Aragonite **Habitat** Epifaunal on shallow soft sediments **Diet** A carnivore

of worms and molluscs **Notes** *Bathytoma haasti*, common in the same age rocks in Canterbury and Otago, is smaller and more finely sculptured. (1 cm)

Phylum Mollusca **Class** Cephalopoda **Family** Aturiidae **Age** Miocene Pl–Tk (18.7–5.3 Ma) **Rock units** Widespread throughout New Zealand **Description** Width 50–200 mm, the last whorl enveloping all previous whorls; sides weakly convex, outer edge strongly and narrowly rounded; suture line between chambers zigzagging strongly to form a deep pocket on each side, then abruptly crossing the outer margin at right angles; face of the septum reveal-

ing the narrow central tube that unites all the chambers **Original shell** Aragonite **Habitat** Swimming near the bottom in deep water **Diet** A predator of fish **Notes** A warm-water group that became extinct at end of Miocene time; related to the living *Nautilus*. (5 cm)

Carcharodon carcharias

Phylum Chordata **Class** Chondrichthyes **Family** Lamnidae **Age** Early Pliocene Wo to living (5.3–0 Ma) **Rock units** Many shallow-water formations **Description** Similar to *Carcharodon megalodon* (see p. 86), but much smaller; height to 50 mm. **Original material** Enamel, dentine **Habitat** Offshore mid-waters **Diet** A predator of fishes and whales **Notes** Teeth of the well-known 'great white shark' are uncommon fossils, easily

recognised by their wide, triangular, symmetrical shape and finely serrated edges; this species possibly evolved from *Carcharodon megalodon*. (1 cm)

Oculina virgosa

Phylum Cnidaria **Class** Anthozoa **Subclass** Zoantharia **Order** Scleractinia **Family** Oculinidae **Age** Early Miocene Po to living (21.7–0 Ma) **Rock units** Deep-water mudstone **Description** Broken fragments of a narrow, branching coral with tree-like growth, 20–30 mm thick, with scattered, alternating coralites along each branch; individual coralites circular, 2–3 mm in width; outer surface around some protruding coralites bearing thin, sharp ridges **Original material** Calcite **Habitat** A colonial, branching coral forming deep-water coral banks **Diet** Filter-feeder **Notes** The growth habit of this coral resembles that of *Lophelia*, but the branches and the outer dense layer of *Oculina* are much thinner and the coralites are much smaller than those of *Lophelia*. (1 cm)

Phylum Arthropoda **Class** Crustacea **Family** Balanidae **Age** Early Pliocene to Early Pleistocene Wo–Wn (5.3–1.6 Ma) **Rock units** Widespread in Wairarapa and Canterbury **Description** Shell to 50 mm high, with six main plates each with six prominent, narrow, irregular longitudinal ribs; plates covering the aperture narrowly triangular, with prominent, deep muscle-insertion pits **Original shell** Calcite **Habitat** Attached to hard objects, notably to *Zygochlamys delicatula* (see p. 115), in offshore waters **Diet** Filter-feeder **Notes** Barnacles have been described as shrimps that lie on their backs and kick food into their mouths with their legs; *Fosterella* is a good example of this shell form; it seems to be a cold-water indicator. (1 cm)

Liothyrella pittensis

Phylum Brachiopoda **Class** Rhynchonellata **Family** Terebratulidae **Age** Pliocene Wo–Wp (5.3–3.0 Ma) **Rock units** Whenuataru Tuff (Pitt Island, Chatham Islands) **Description** Length 30–40 mm, evenly oval, smooth, inflated, with a relatively long, narrow beak and an unusually large pedicle foramen **Original shell** Calcite **Habitat** Attached by its pedicle to hard objects in shallow water **Diet** Filter-feeder **Notes** This moderately large, smooth brachiopod is common on Pitt Island. The genus *Liothyrella* is easily recognised by its larger pedicle foramen, longer beak and less vertically compressed shape than those of the similar smooth brachiopods *Pachymagas* (see p. 90) and *Neothyris* (see next entry). (1 cm)

Neothyris obtusa

Phylum Brachiopoda **Class** Rhynchonellata **Family** Terebratellidae **Age** Late Pliocene to Early Pleistocene Wm–Wn (3.0–1.6 Ma)
Rock units Castlepoint Formation (Castlepoint), and other limestone formations in the eastern North Island **Description** Length
35–45 mm, smooth, evenly oval, without flexures of the valve
margins; beak rather small, and pedicle foramen very small and not
functional in adults **Original shell** Calcite **Habitat** Lying loose on
the seabed in current-swept environments **Diet** Filter-feeder **Notes**
Neothyris has a thickened area in the lower valve and a thinner,
rather fragile pedicle valve, and the shell lies loose when adult; the

thickened area acts
as a counterweight,
allowing the shell
to right itself after
rolling around in
currents. (1 cm)

Notosaria nigricans

Phylum Brachiopoda **Class** Rhynchonellata **Family** Notosariidae
Age Early Miocene Pl to living (18.7–0 Ma) **Rock units** Many
shallow-water formations **Description** Length 15–25 mm, width
much greater than height, with a long, weakly curved anterior margin,
a strongly protruding beak, and an evenly curved posterior margin;
pedicle foramen large, triangular, with straight margin against the upper
valve; sculpture of many narrow radial ribs and a shallow sulcus flexing
the posterior valve margin; fossil specimens are silvery-looking, or retain
the original black colour **Original shell** Calcite **Habitat** Attached by
its pedicle to hard objects in shallow water **Diet** Filter-feeder **Notes**
This is the common, still living 'ribbed black brachiopod'. (1 cm)

Phylum Mollusca **Class** Bivalvia **Family** Ostreidae **Age** Late Miocene to Early Pleistocene Tt–early Wn (11–2.4 Ma) **Rock units** Widespread in near-shore formations **Description** Height 200 mm to more than 300 mm, very thick, most specimens tall and narrow; lower valve shallowly cupped, upper valve flat; sculpture of low commarginal ridges only; single adductor muscle scar almost square, with an embayed dorsal margin, purplish red in many specimens **Original shell** Calcite **Habitat** Cemented to hard objects, or forming reefs in shallow water **Diet** Filter-feeder **Notes** This huge, thick, long, narrow oyster is a useful age index that became extinct at about 2.4 Ma. (5 cm)

Glycymerita (Manaia) manaiaensis

Phylum Mollusca **Class** Bivalvia **Family** Glycymerididae **Age** Pliocene to Early Pleistocene Wp–early Wn (3.6–2 Ma) **Rock units** Widespread in near-shore rocks **Description** Height 50–60 mm, evenly oval, with low beaks; sculpture of 35–38 shallow, widely spaced radial grooves; hinge with many similar curved teeth, obliterated in the centre of the hinge; ligamental area without grooves; ventral margin coarsely crenulate **Original shell** Aragonite **Habitat** Burrowing shallowly in soft sediments **Diet** Filter-feeder **Notes** This distinctive, oval glycymerid is easily recognised by the lack of ligamental grooves on the triangular area below the beak. (1 cm)

Phialopecten thomsoni

Phylum Mollusca **Class** Bivalvia **Family** Pectinidae **Age** Late Pliocene to earliest Pleistocene Wm–early Wn (3.0–2.0 Ma) **Rock units** Common in limestone and shellbeds **Description** Height 100–175 mm, slightly wider than high; auricles large; sculpture of 18–20 prominent radial ribs, wide and weakly convex with many grooves on the right valve, high and narrow on the left valve **Original shell** Calcite **Habitat** Lying free on shallow, soft sediments **Diet** Filter-feeder **Notes** The largest of a lineage of scallops useful for dating rocks; *Phialopecten marwicki* (Wc–Wp, 5.3–3.0 Ma) has 28–30 less finely divided ribs; *P. triphooki* (early Wn, 2.4–2.2 Ma) is smaller and has a deep groove down the centre of each rib. (5 cm)

Mesopeplum crawfordi

Phylum Mollusca **Class** Bivalvia **Family** Pectinidae **Age** Pliocene Wo–Wp (5.3–3.0 Ma); similar forms as old as Middle Miocene Sw (13–11 Ma) **Rock units** Widespread in near-shore rocks **Description** Height 70–125 mm, length slightly greater than height; right valve strongly convex, left valve almost flat; auricles square, relatively small; sculptured with five very prominent radial folds, fading out down the shell, and many prominent, narrow, closely spaced radial riblets **Original shell** Calcite **Habitat** Lying free on soft sediments

Diet Filter-feeder **Notes** Easily recognised because of its large size, prominent radial folds, and flat left valve; the much smaller species *Mesopeplum convexum*, with evenly inflated valves, is abundant at Castlepoint. (5 cm)

Phylum Mollusca **Class** Bivalvia **Family** Cardiidae **Age** Late Miocene to Late Pliocene Tt–Wm (11–2.4 Ma) **Rock units** Widespread in shallow-water rocks **Description** Length 135–155 mm, highly inflated, thick, triangularly elongate; sculptured with 40 prominent radial ribs, the posterior six lower and more closely spaced than the others; large pointed nodules on the ribs near the ends; hinge with prominent, pointed central teeth, large anterior lateral and small posterior lateral teeth, ligamental plate very prominent, wide, smooth; ventral margin crenulate **Original shell** Aragonite **Habitat** Shallow burrower in soft sediments **Diet** Filter-feeder **Notes** One of the largest 'cockles' (Cardiidae) in the world, easily recognised by its thick shell, inflated shape and prominent radial ribs. (5 cm)

Mactra (Maorimactra) chrydaea

Phylum Mollusca **Class** Bivalvia **Family** Mactridae **Age** Late Miocene to mid-Pliocene Tk–Wp (7.2–3.0 Ma) **Rock units** Common in shallow-water formations; abundant in Birch's Mill shell lens (Te Waewae Bay, Southland) **Description** Length 17–28 mm, very inflated, length greater than height; exterior smooth except for growth ridges; hinge with two small central teeth in the right valve, a bilobed central tooth in the left valve, and thick lateral teeth in both valves; ventral margin smooth **Original shell** Aragonite **Habitat** Burrowing shallowly in soft sediments **Diet** Filter-feeder **Notes** This small, very inflated *Mactra* species is a useful age indicator in latest Miocene and early Pliocene rocks. (1 cm)

Pelicaria canaliculata

Phylum Mollusca **Class** Gastropoda **Family** Struthiolariidae **Age** Mid-Pliocene Wp (3.6–3.0 Ma) **Rock units** Common in Starborough Formation (Awatere Valley, Marlborough), northern Wairarapa and South Taranaki coast **Description** Height 38–55 mm, with a deep sutural channel; aperture with relatively narrow lips; sculpture of extremely prominent spiral cords with convex crests and deeply undercut edges, three to four on spire whorls and eight on the last whorl **Original**

shell Aragonite **Habitat** Shallow sandy sediments, burrowing shallowly to feed **Diet** A ciliary deposit-feeder, gathering particles from the seafloor **Notes** The prominent spiral ribs make this species very easily recognised; it has a shallower sutural channel and coarser sculpture than *Pelicaria zelandiae* (Wp, 3.6–3.0 Ma). (1 cm)

Alcithoe gatesi

Phylum Mollusca **Class** Gastropoda **Family** Volutidae **Age** Pliocene Wp–Wm? (3.6–2.4 Ma) **Rock units** Shallow-water formations along the Taranaki–Wanganui coast and in Hawke's Bay **Description** Height 45–55 mm, tall and narrow, with a weakly concave sutural ramp and a parallel-sided last whorl; sculpture of many long, narrow, sharp-crested axial ribs descending onto the last whorl; aperture with smooth, thickened lips; the columella bears four narrow folds **Original shell** Aragonite **Habitat** Shallow sandy sediments, partially buried **Diet** Carnivore feeding on bivalves **Notes** Late Miocene–Pliocene volutes have coarser axial ribs than any living species, such as *Alcithoe arabica* (see p. 126). (1 cm)

Phylum Mollusca **Class** Gastropoda **Family** Pseudotomidae **Age** Pliocene Wo–Wp (5.3–3.0 Ma) **Rock units** Many shallow-water rocks **Description** Height 40–45 mm, spire stepped by the prominent, concave sutural ramp; last whorl tapering a little to the anterior end, with a widely open siphonal canal; sculpture of prominent, rounded

axial ribs crossed by low, wide, spiral riblets, and many fine, closely spaced, spiral threads **Original shell** Aragonite **Habitat** Epifaunal on soft sediments **Diet** A carnivore feeding on molluscs and worms **Notes** One of the youngest species in a restricted New Zealand genus, identifiable by their wide anterior end and their sculpture of fine spiral threads overriding all other sculpture. (1 cm)

Gemmaterebra bicorona

Phylum Mollusca **Class** Gastropoda **Family** Terebridae **Age** Middle Miocene–Late Pliocene Sl–Wm (15.1–2.4 Ma) **Rock Units** Widespread in shallow-water formations **Description** Height 40–60 mm, tall and narrow, with sinuous whorl outlines; last whorl short, with a narrow siphonal canal; sculpture of two rows of low nodules around the top of each whorl, fine spiral threads lower on each whorl, and a protruding ridge above the strongly rounded base **Original shell** Aragonite **Habitat** Shallowly buried in soft sediments **Diet** A carnivore of infaunal molluscs **Notes** One of few New Zealand members of a diverse tropical family of infaunal carnivores. (1 cm)

Kingdom Plantae **Family** Lauraceae **Age** Pleistocene to Recent Wc–living (1.63–0 Ma) **Rock units** Mangatuna Formation (Ormond, Gisborne) **Description** A small simple angiosperm leaf with smooth margin, short and narrow petiole, and narrow midvein; the secondary veins are faint, depart the midvein at a moderately wide angle and curve upwards towards margin **Notes** The Lauraceae were an important part of the New Zealand flora from Late Cretaceous to Miocene time, but there are only three genera in the modern New Zealand flora; the pollen of Lauraceae rarely preserves and so macrofossils and mesofossils (dispersed cuticle and tiny flowers) are important. (1 cm)

Plagianthus betulinus

Kingdom Plantae **Family** Malvaceae **Age** Pleistocene to Recent Wc–living (1.63–0 Ma) **Rock units** Mangatuna Formation (Ormond, Gisborne) **Description** A small angiosperm leaf with prominent serrated margin, acute apex and rounded base **Notes** This specimen was originally described as *Nothofagus fusca* (red beech) but was reassigned to *Plagianthus betulinus* (ribbonwood). (1 cm)

CENOZOIC: QUATERNARY / PLEISTOCENE

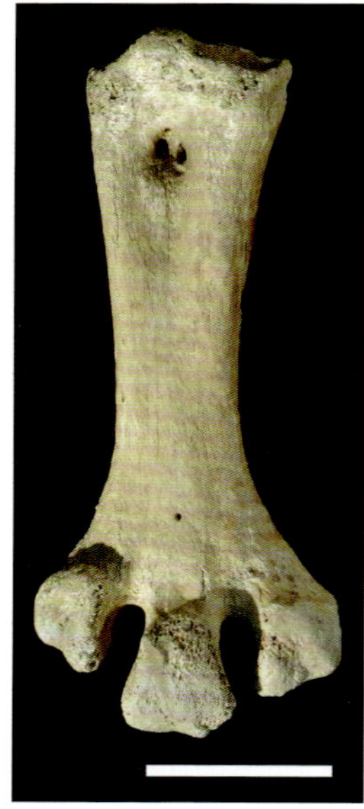

PLEISTOCENE

CENOZOIC: QUATERNARY

Phylum Chordata **Class** Aves **Family** Dinornithidae **Age** Holocene Wq (less than 1000 years) **Rock units** Abundant in swamp and cave deposits **Description** The tarsometatarsal bone, about 200 mm long, of a moderately large moa (known as the upland moa), originally about 1.3 m tall, showing the articulation points for the three toe bones at the lower end, and the articulation for the upper, long leg bone (femur) at the top **Original material** Apatite **Habitat** A flightless grazer of forest margins and tussock **Diet** Trees and shrubs **Notes** An example of a distinctive bone from the extinct New Zealand moa, with three ankle bones fused to the lower leg bone. (5 cm)

Prototroctes oxyrhynchus

Phylum Chordata **Class** Osteichthyes **Family** Retropinnidae **Age** Pleistocene Wc (0.6 Ma) **Rock unit** Ormond Valley lake deposit (Gisborne) **Description** The skeleton of a fish, 125 mm long, with clearly visible skull, vertebrae, ribs, tail and some fins **Original material** Apatite **Habitat** Freshwater streams **Diet** Unknown **Notes** This fossil of the extinct New Zealand 'grayling' is an example of a fossil New Zealand freshwater fish; this species formerly was abundant in New Zealand streams, but became extinct early in the twentieth century. The bone has been dissolved away, leaving a mould, which reveals many details because it is preserved in a fine-grained white diatomite. (5 cm)

Monomyces rubrum

Phylum Cnidaria **Class** Anthozoa **Subclass** Zoantharia **Order** Scleractinia **Family** Flabellidae **Age** Late Miocene Tk to living (7.2–0 Ma) **Rock units** Many shallow-water formations **Description** Height 5–45 mm, width 6–100 mm, angle between the sides 24°–125°; oval in plan, with evenly rounded edges; attached to hard objects by an obvious scar or narrow pedicle; surface smooth or roughened **Original material** Calcite **Habitat** Attached to hard objects in environments with no sediment **Diet** Filter-feeder **Notes** The most common solitary coral in shallow water around New Zealand at present, e.g. living under low-tidal boulders in some sheltered Northland bays, and is an uncommon fossil at Wanganui and at Te Piki, East Cape. (1 cm)

Trichopeltarion greggi

Phylum Arthropoda **Class** Crustacea **Family** Atelecyclidae **Age** Early Pleistocene Wn (2.4–1.6 Ma) **Rock units** Debris flows, Motunau Beach (Canterbury) **Description** Carapace 70 mm wide (including spines), subcircular, with six large spines and many small, narrow spines around the outline; most of the surface bears small, sharp spines; the legs are short, with a large, wide right pincer but a small, narrow left pincer **Original shell** Calcium phosphate **Habitat** Offshore soft sediments **Diet** Scavenger **Notes** Similar to the living species *Trichopeltarion fantasticum*, which lives in 15–750 m on soft sediments around central and southern New Zealand; other shallow-water crabs such as *Cancer* also occur as fossils at Motunau. (5 cm)

Calloria inconspicua

Phylum Brachiopoda **Family** Terebratellidae **Age** Late Pliocene Wm to living (3.0–0 Ma) **Rock units** Common in many formations **Description** Length 10–15 mm, almost evenly oval, height greater than length, smooth apart from a wide, shallow central sulcus in the lower valve and a corresponding depression in the upper (pedicle) valve, producing a shallow flexure of the valve margins; upper valve protruding at the beak to form a spout with a large, circular pedicle foramen **Original shell** Calcite **Habitat** Attached by its pedicle to the undersides of rocks in shallow water **Diet** Filter-feeder **Notes** The common little red 'finger-nail' brachiopod living in the intertidal zone around New Zealand. (1 cm)

Terebratella sanguinea

Phylum Brachiopoda **Family** Terebratellidae **Age** Late Pliocene Wm to living (3.0–0 Ma) **Rock units** Common in many shallow-water formations **Description** Length 20–30 mm, oval, with prominent sculpture of 20–30 narrow radial ribs, increasing in number by inserting further ribs as the shell grows; a wide, shallow sulcus in the lower valve and matching fold in the pedicle valve produce a shallow flexure of the valve margin; the pedicle foramen is moderately large **Original shell** Calcite **Habitat** Attached by its pedicle to hard objects in shallow water **Diet** Filter-feeder **Notes** This large, radially ribbed 'red brachiopod' is common today in central and southern New Zealand. (1 cm)

Pecten novaezelandiae

Phylum Mollusca **Class** Bivalvia **Family** Pectinidae **Age** Pleistocene mid-Wc to living (1.1–0 Ma) **Rock units** Common in shellbeds in Wanganui Basin and at Te Piki (East Cape) **Description** Length 100–140 mm, right (lower) valve bowl-shaped, left (upper) valve flat

to weakly concave; auricles square, symmetrical; sculpture of 20–22 flat-topped to evenly convex radial ribs, wide on the right valve, narrow on the left valve **Original shell** Calcite **Habitat** Lying free on soft sediments, excavated into a shallow hollow with the flat valve at the sediment surface **Diet** Filter-feeder **Notes** The familiar edible scallop, easily identified by its one cupped and one flat valve. (5 cm)

Zygochlamys delicatula

Phylum Mollusca **Class** Bivalvia **Family** Pectinidae **Age** Early Pleistocene Wn to living (2.4–0 Ma) **Rock units** Abundant in deep-water shellbeds in Wanganui Basin, eastern North Island and North Canterbury **Description** Height 50–95 mm, almost circular, with small auricles; sculpture of prominent, scaly radial ribs; ribs low, wide and each bearing two to three riblets on the right valve, but narrow-crested and with wide concave interspaces on the left valve **Original shell** Calcite **Habitat** Lying free on soft sediments in more than 100 m of water **Diet** Filter-feeder **Notes** An indicator of glacial conditions in the past, living now in deep water in southern New Zealand and more shallowly in the subantarctic. (1 cm)

Phylum Mollusca **Class** Bivalvia **Family** Pectinidae **Age** Late Oligocene Ld? to living (27–0 Ma) **Rock units** Abundant in many rocks throughout New Zealand **Description** Height 30–65 mm, thin, brittle, very weakly inflated; height greater than length; slightly obliquely elongate postero-ventrally; posterior auricles very small, inclined forwards; anterior auricles large, the right one with a deep byssal notch; disc sculpture of 25–35 or more high, narrow, finely scaly radial ribs, with still narrower riblets in their interspaces **Original shell** Calcite **Habitat** Byssally attached to hard objects in 0–800+ m of water **Diet** Filter-feeder **Notes** One of the most ecologically tolerant of New Zealand molluscs, occurring commonly in most fully marine rocks. (1 cm)

Ostrea chilensis

Phylum Mollusca **Class** Bivalvia **Family** Ostreidae **Age** Late Miocene Tt to living (11–0 Ma) **Rock units** Abundant in a huge variety of rocks **Description** Height 30–120 mm, lower (left) valve shallowly cupped, upper (right) valve flat; sculpture highly variable depending on the environment, specimens living on sand and mud with obvious, wide frills on the lower valve; upper valve weakly sculptured; single adductor muscle scar crescentic, slightly in front of the centre of the valve **Original shell** Calcite **Habitat** Lying free on soft sediments in offshore current-swept environments and, less commonly, cemented to rocks and shells **Diet** Filter-feeder **Notes** The common living 'Bluff oyster', dredged now throughout New Zealand. (5 cm)

Patro undatus

Phylum Mollusca **Class** Bivalvia **Family** Anomiidae **Age** Late Miocene to Early Pleistocene Tk–Wn (7.2–1.6 Ma) **Rock units** Many shallow-water formations **Description** Height 60–100 mm, oyster-like, circular; left valve weakly inflated, composed of platy

calcite, interior with three muscle scars inside the white (aragonitic) central area, the lowest scar the largest; right valve prismatic, flat, interior with one muscle scar, a calcified brown byssal plug, and a prominent ligamental attachment surface **Original shell** Calcite **Habitat** Cemented by its calcified byssus to hard objects in shallow water **Diet** Filter-feeder **Notes** One of several distinctive bivalves whose extinction marks the end of Nukumaruan time (1.63 Ma); *Anomia* is smaller, and has the uppermost muscle scar the largest. (5 cm)

Lutraria grandis

Phylum Mollusca **Class** Bivalvia **Family** Mactridae **Age** Pliocene to Early Pleistocene Wo–Wn (5.3–1.6 Ma) **Rock units** Common in near-shore rocks in Wanganui Basin, Waiouru, eastern North Island and North Canterbury **Description** Length 110–140 mm, elongate, with beaks at the anterior third of the length; dorsal and ventral margins diverging towards the posterior; posterior end gaping widely; exterior smooth except for weak wrinkles; hinge with small teeth and a large, spoon-shaped ligamental pit **Original shell** Aragonite **Habitat** Burrowing deeply in sand **Diet** Filter-feeder **Notes** This large bivalve is another of the distinctive molluscs that became extinct at the end of Nukumaruan time (1.63 Ma). (1 cm)

Phylum Mollusca **Class** Bivalvia **Family** Tellinidae **Age** Pliocene to Pleistocene Wp–Wq (3.6–0.3 Ma) **Rock units** Estuarine mudstone throughout New Zealand **Description** Length 28–35 mm, thick-shelled, exterior smooth; anterior end evenly rounded, posterior end with an obvious twist to the right, forming a ridge parallel to the posterior dorsal margin; hinge with a very large, prominent, triangular central tooth in the right valve and two narrower teeth in the left valve, and a thick posterior lateral tooth in each valve **Original shell** Aragonite **Habitat** Burrowing deeply in estuarine tidal flats **Diet** Filter-feeder **Notes** This very distinctive, restricted New Zealand genus became extinct only about 300,000 years ago. (1 cm)

Eumarcia plana

Phylum Mollusca **Class** Bivalvia **Family** Veneridae **Age** Pliocene to Early Pleistocene Wp–Wn (3.6–1.6 Ma) **Rock units** Shallow-water sands in Wanganui Basin, eastern North Island, North Canterbury, and Titirangi (Chatham Islands) **Description** Length 60–100 mm, evenly oval, rather thin-shelled, exterior smooth; beaks low, at anterior quarter of the length; ventral margin smooth; hinge with three narrow, grooved central teeth in each valve **Original shell** Aragonite **Habitat** Burrowing shallowly in soft sediments **Diet** Filter-feeder **Notes** Similar to but much larger than living southern Australian species of *Eumarcia*; another of the distinctive molluscs extinct in New Zealand at the end of Nukumaruan time (1.63 Ma). (1 cm)

Tawera subsulcata

Phylum Mollusca **Class** Bivalvia **Family** Veneridae **Age** Early Pleistocene Wn (2.4–1.6 Ma) **Rock units** Abundant in near-shore rocks in Wanganui Basin, eastern North Island and North Canterbury **Description** Length 25–35 mm, evenly oval, thick-shelled; ventral margin finely crenulate; exterior sculptured with prominent, convex-crested commarginal ridges, with flat interspaces each about half the width of one ridge; hinge with three narrow central teeth in each valve **Original shell** Aragonite **Habitat** Burrowing shallowly in soft sediments **Diet** Filter-feeder **Notes** Very similar to the living and common fossil species *Tawera spissa*, but the ridges are more closely spaced in all other *Tawera* species. (1 cm)

Austrovenus stutchburyi

Phylum Mollusca **Class** Bivalvia **Family** Veneridae **Age** Pliocene Wo to living (5.3–0 Ma) **Rock units** Estuarine rocks throughout New Zealand **Description** Length 15–65 mm, thick-shelled; oval, weakly triangular or subcircular, with beaks protruding strongly in some forms; ventral margin finely crenulate; exterior sculptured with both low, flat-topped radial ridges and prominent, narrow commarginal lamellae; hinge with three prominent central teeth in each valve, and a round anterior lateral tooth in the right valve **Original shell** Aragonite **Habitat** Burrowing very shallowly in estuarine tidal flats **Diet** Filter-feeder **Notes** The most abundant shell fossil in New Zealand, occurring in enormous numbers in raised beach deposits and young shellbeds. (1 cm)

Barnea similis

Phylum Mollusca **Class** Bivalvia **Family** Pholadidae **Age** Late Miocene Tt to living (11–0 Ma) **Rock units** Widespread throughout New Zealand **Description** Length 65–100 mm, cylindrical, tapering slightly to the posterior end; anterior end deeply embayed for protrusion of the foot, posterior end oval; exterior sculpture of serrated radial ribs on the anterior end, otherwise weak; anterior adductor muscle scar situated on an out-rolled dorsal margin; hinge with a single narrow rod supporting the ligament in each valve **Original shell** Aragonite **Habitat** Boring in soft rocks low in the

intertidal zone and subtidally **Diet** Filter-feeder **Notes** Found commonly in its bore-holes on unconformity surfaces at Wanganui. (1 cm)

Zethalia zelandica

Phylum Mollusca **Class** Gastropoda **Family** Trochidae **Age** Early Pleistocene Wn to living (2.4–0 Ma) **Rock units** Common in shallow-water sands **Description** Width 15–23 mm, with very low, conical, flat-sided spire, narrowly bi-angled sides, and an almost flat base with a completely plugged umbilicus; sculpture of weak radial grooves around the umbilicus and fine spiral ridges on the base; surface smooth and polished; aperture rectangular **Original shell** Aragonite **Habitat** Active wave zone off sandy ocean beaches,

in 3–5 m of water **Diet** Particle-sorting deposit-feeder **Notes** A useful indicator of sandy ocean beach conditions; many specimens retain a pink and purple colour pattern. (1 cm)

Taxonia suteri

Phylum Mollusca **Class** Gastropoda **Family** Cerithiidae **Age** Late Pliocene to Early Pleistocene Wm–Wn (3.0–1.6 Ma) **Rock units** Estuarine sands in Wanganui and Hawke's Bay **Description** Height 10–18 mm, tall and narrow, with sculpture of closely spaced, coin-shaped nodules, three rows on spire whorls and six to seven on the last whorl; aperture with a short siphonal canal, three prominent spiral ridges inside the outer lip, two high up on the inner lip and one on the base of the columella **Original shell** Aragonite **Habitat** Creeping on estuarine tidal flats, probably in mangroves **Diet** Deposit-feeder

Notes A restricted New Zealand estuarine 'mud-creeper'; another distinctive mollusc that became extinct at the end of Nukumaruan time (1.63 Ma). (1 cm)

CENOZOIC: QUATERNARY

PLEISTOCENE

Stiracolpus symmetricus

Phylum Mollusca **Class** Gastropoda **Family** Turritellidae **Age** Early Pleistocene Wn to living (2.4–0 Ma) **Rock units** Abundant in many formations **Description** Height 20–30 mm, tall and narrowly conical, with flat to strongly convex whorl sides, a flat base and a rectangular aperture; sculpture of prominent, smooth, convex spiral ribs, very variable in number, three on most specimens outer lip with a wide, V-shaped sinus in the centre **Original shell** Aragonite **Habitat** Shallowly buried in soft sediments **Diet** A ciliary deposit-feeder, gathering particles from the seafloor **Notes** Highly varied in the shape of the whorl profile and the strength of the spiral cords. (1 cm)

PLEISTOCENE

CENOZOIC: QUATERNARY

Phylum Mollusca **Class** Gastropoda **Family** Turritellidae **Age** Early Pliocene Wo to living (5.3–0 Ma) **Rock units** Abundant in many formations **Description** Height 50–80 mm, tall and narrowly conical, but relatively broad for a New Zealand turritellid; whorl sides almost flat; sculpture of low, narrow spiral ribs, five to six higher on the whorl and a group of two to three closely spaced around the lower part of each whorl; base flat, aperture rectangular; outer lip with a wide, V-shaped sinus in the centre **Original shell** Aragonite **Habitat** Shallowly buried in soft sediments **Diet** A ciliary deposit-feeder, gathering particles from the seafloor **Notes** Much the most common New Zealand turritellid, occurring in all soft-bottom environments. (1 cm)

Struthiolaria frazeri

Phylum Mollusca **Class** Gastropoda **Family** Struthiolariidae **Age** Late Pliocene to Early Pleistocene Wm–Wn (3.0–1.6 Ma) **Rock units** Sandstone in Hawke's Bay **Description** Height 70–100 mm, with strongly shouldered whorls; aperture circular, with thick, smooth lips, outer lip sinuous; sculpture of prominent, wide spiral ribs of square cross-section, three on the sutural ramp, a prominent one forming the shoulder angle, bearing nodules on many specimens, four ribs on whorl sides, and a further six or seven on the base **Original shell** Aragonite **Habitat** Shallow soft sediments, burrowing shallowly to feed **Diet** A ciliary deposit-feeder, gathering particles from the seafloor **Notes** The largest struthiolariid, easily recognised by its tall spire and prominent spiral cords. (1 cm)

Struthiolaria papulosa

Phylum Mollusca **Class** Gastropoda **Family** Struthiolariidae **Age** Early Pleistocene Wn to living (2.4–0 Ma) **Rock units** Many near-shore formations **Description** Height 70–90 mm, with a strongly stepped spire, a short last whorl and an oval aperture with thick, smooth, sinuous lips; sculpture of small to prominent nodules round the shoulder angle, and many low, flat-topped spiral cords over the entire exterior **Original shell**

Aragonite **Habitat** Shallow soft sediments, shallow burrower **Diet** A ciliary deposit-feeder, gathering particles from the seafloor **Notes** This tall specimen from Castlecliff, Wanganui, is the '*gigas* form' with weak nodules and a tall spire, living now at Stewart Island, indicating cool temperatures at the time of deposition. (5 cm)

Pelicaria vermis

Phylum Mollusca **Class** Gastropoda **Family** Struthiolariidae **Age** Early Pleistocene Wn to living (2.4–0 Ma) **Rock units** Many shallow-water formations **Description** Height 40–58 mm, whorls evenly inflated; sutural ramp narrow and horizontal to narrowly channelled; sculpture of a few low, wide spiral ribs, very subdued to high and prominent; aperture with thick, smooth lips, the outer lip sinuous **Original shell** Aragonite **Habitat** Shallow soft sediments, burrowing shallowly to feed **Diet** A ciliary deposit-feeder, gathering particles from the seafloor **Notes** Variable in the prominence of the

spiral ribs; strongly ribbed specimens occurred in cool water in South Wairarapa, and are found now only in water more than 200 m deep. (1 cm)

Phylum Mollusca **Class** Gastropoda **Family** Buccinulidae **Age** Early Pleistocene Wn to living (2.4–0 Ma) **Rock units** Offshore siltstone in Marlborough and North Canterbury **Description** Height 45–65 mm, last whorl short and narrow, sutural ramp strongly concave; sculpture of closely spaced, rounded axial ribs, fading out on the last whorl; crossed by rounded spiral cords, forming small nodules where they meet; siphonal canal short, forming a prominent fasciole bordered by a sharp rib **Original shell** Aragonite **Habitat** Epifaunal on soft sediments **Diet** A scavenger **Notes** Along

with *Zygochlamys delicatula* (see p. 115), this species is an indicator of cool sea temperatures, living now mainly around the southern South Island and subantarctic islands. (1 cm)

Austrofusus glans

Phylum Mollusca **Class** Gastropoda **Family** Buccinulidae **Age** Pleistocene Wc to living (1.6–0 Ma) **Rock units** Common in shellbeds at Castlecliff, Wanganui **Description** Height 50–80 mm, with a strongly stepped spire, a rectangular last whorl, a long, weakly twisted siphonal canal and a low but obvious fasciole; sculpture of one row of sharp nodules at the shoulder angle, another row of smaller nodules around the lower angulation, and many narrow spiral cords all over

Original shell Aragonite **Habitat** Epifaunal on soft sediments in shallow to deep water **Diet** A generalised carnivore and scavenger **Notes** Much the most abundant 'whelk' in New Zealand; this genus has a long, complex evolutionary history. (1 cm)

Poirieria zelandica

Phylum Mollusca **Class** Gastropoda **Family** Muricidae **Age** Early Pliocene Wo to living (5.3–0 Ma) **Rock units** Common in offshore siltstone **Description** Height 40–65 mm, with a stepped spire and a circular aperture; sculpture of a row of long, horizontal, open spines around the shoulder angle, forming a weakly concave sutural ramp, and four rows of shorter spines below, protruding from the outer lip; former siphonal canals are united into a further row of spines surrounding the false umbilicus **Original shell** Aragonite **Habitat** Epifaunal on soft sediments **Diet** A generalised carnivore **Notes** The most common New Zealand 'spiny murex' shell, easily recognised by the row of long shoulder spines. (1 cm)

Aeneator marshalli

Phylum Mollusca **Class** Gastropoda **Family** Buccinulidae **Age** Early Pleistocene Wn to living (2 4–0 Ma) **Rock units** Offshore siltstone at Castlecliff (Wanganui) **Description** Height 50–80 mm, tall and narrow, with a relatively short spire, evenly and strongly inflated whorls, and a long, straight, open siphonal canal; sculpture of many narrow, closely spaced spiral and axial riblets, without nodules **Original shell** Aragonite **Habitat** Epifaunal on soft sediments

Diet A generalised carnivore **Notes** Easily recognised by its rather short spire, long siphonal canal and rounded whorls; *Penion* species (see e.g. p. 100) reach a much larger size, and *Buccinulum* species are smaller and have a shorter siphonal canal. (1 cm)

Phylum Mollusca **Class** Gastropoda **Family** Volutidae **Age** Early Pleistocene Wn to living (2.4–0 Ma) **Rock units** Widespread throughout New Zealand **Description** Height 100–180 mm, with a short to moderately tall spire, a long, parallel-sided last whorl and a long, narrow aperture; sculpture of a row of sharp nodules at the shoulder angle in some specimens, very variable in size and prominence; inner lip with a flat plate protruding along the left edge; columella bearing four prominent folds **Original shell** Aragonite **Habitat** Shallow soft sediments, partially buried **Diet** Carnivore, feeding on bivalves **Notes** Variable in the size and prominence of the shoulder nodules; many named forms intergrade. (1 cm)

Amalda (Baryspira) mucronata

Phylum Mollusca **Class** Gastropoda **Family** Olividae **Age** Early Pleistocene Wn to living (2.4–0 Ma) **Rock units** Many shallow-water formations **Description** Height 30–70 mm, narrowly oval, with a smooth, evenly inflated spire and a parallel-sided last whorl; depressed spiral band around last whorl narrow but obvious, other bands and grooves weakly defined; columella with up to nine narrow spiral ridges **Original shell** Aragonite **Habitat** Creeping, partly buried in soft sediments, with its broad foot expanded **Diet** Carnivore, feeding on bivalves **Notes** The largest New Zealand 'olive shell', with a thicker, more inflated spire callus than the shallow-water species *Amalda australis*; much larger than other young species. (1 cm)

Phylum Mollusca **Class** Gastropoda **Family** Amathinidae **Age** Early Pleistocene latest Wn to living (1.7–0 Ma) **Rock units** Common in many shellbeds at Castlecliff (Wanganui) and Te Piki (East Cape) **Description** Height 15–27 mm, oval, inflated, with a tall, weakly stepped spire and a large, long last whorl with an evenly rounded anterior end; surface smooth except for many narrow, punctate spiral grooves; aperture narrow, widening anteriorly, with a single low fold on the columella **Original shell** Aragonite **Habitat** Epifaunal on shallow-water sand flats **Diet** A parasite of shallow-water bivalves, probably mainly *Austrovenus stutchburyi* (see p. 119) in New Zealand. (5 mm)

Pseudo-fossils

Fossils are recognised on the basis of such features as shape, size, texture, structure and colour. However, there are plenty of things in nature that can fool us. Here are examples of three features that are commonly mistaken for fossils.

1. Sedimentary features such as ripples: Regular, often shapely curved features may relate to current-flow processes acting on the soft, movable sediment on the seafloor, normally sand, silt and mud. Patterns can be generated that are subsequently preserved in the rock and appear to be very organic-looking, as if part of an animal or plant.

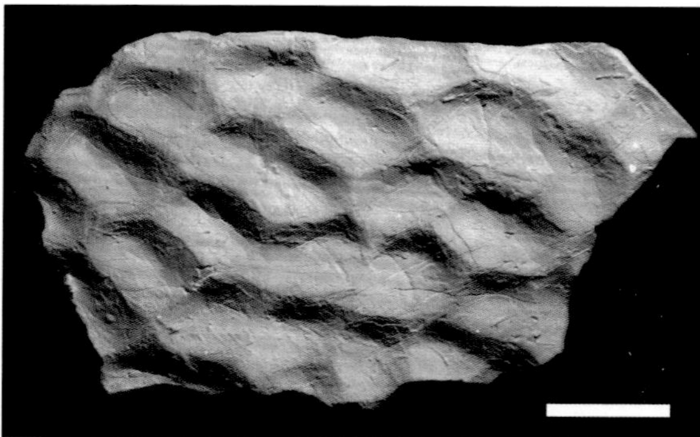

Ripples (5 cm)

2. Mineral growths: Rock surfaces are often discoloured and may reveal highly organised patterns that can look very like the fronds of a fern or some other leaf fossil. The photo shows an example of just

Mineral growth (1 cm)

that. In fact it is dendritic growth of an iron- and manganese-rich hydroxide mineral that grew on the surface of a fracture or crack within the rock. These are very common. Usually, these mineral growths form long after the rock was formed so they are therefore referred to as 'secondary' mineral growths. The mineral grows as a precipitate, usually from an evaporating percolating fluid that happens to be bearing iron and manganese. Mineral growths are best observed on a pale-coloured rock, but can of course occur on any rock (igneous, sedimentary or metamorphic).

3. Structural features: Regular patterns generated by unusual natural 'packing phenomena' can produce highly organised structures that look organic, as if they must be part of the remains of a plant or animal. One of the more common is referred to by geologists as 'cone-in-cone structure'. The rock looks as though it is composed of a whole lot of neatly stacked V-shaped or W-shaped cones. In fact, they are rhythmically arranged parallel or subparallel fractures that develop in very fine-grained clay-rich sediments (muds). Their origin is to do with preferred orientation of clay minerals (which are microscopic) under specific pressure constraints; the amount of water present is also a factor. These structures are surprisingly common, especially in mudstones, siltstones and concretions.

Cone-in-cone structure (1 cm)

Glossary

agglutinated composed of sand or silt grains that are cemented or 'glued' together.
allometric growth the relationship between size and shape, which changes with growth.
ammonite a Mesozoic ammonoid group with an ammonitic suture.
ammonoid extinct group of cephalopod molluscs.
aperture the opening or mouth of a tubular shell as in a gastropod, nautiloid or ammonoid.
aragonite a mineral of calcium carbonate with a crystal structure that differs from calcite.
auricle a flat triangular ear-like or wing-like extension of the bivalve shell hinge.
beak extremity of the brachiopod umbo, commonly pointed.
belemnite an extinct group of squid-like cephalopods.
bifurcate split in two.
biogenic produced by a living organism; of biological origin.
bivalve a mollusc shell with two valves, left valve and right, connected by a ligament.
brachiopod a shell with two valves, dorsal and ventral, that are interlocked at the hinge.
bryozoan a colonial sessile animal group with a calcite skeleton.
byssus the mass of tough hair-like fibres that attach a bivalve to the substrate.
calcite a mineral of calcium carbonate with a crystal structure that differs from aragonite.
capillate bearing capillae: fine radial threads on the shell surface.
carinae prominent ridges on a shell.
cephalopod marine mollusc of the class Cephalopoda; includes octopuses and squids.
colony a group of animals (or plants) of the same species that live closely packed together.
columella the central shelly spiral column developed in gastropods.
commarginal parallel to the shell margin.
comminuted broken into small fragments.
conodonts tooth-like structures from the jaws of a group of primitive eel-like fish.
corallum the part of the coral the animal lives in.
costae prominent radial ribs or ridges on a shell.
costellae fine radial ornament on a shell; less prominent than costae.
crura the sturdy branch-like shelly processes that support the loop of a brachiopod.
deposit-feeder feeding on organic matter trapped in sediment.
edentulous lacking hinge teeth, particularly in bivalves.
equant of equal dimensions with respect to the location of the umbo or beak.
equivalve a bivalve body plan in which both valves appear the same.

evolute where the spiral coil or whorl of a mollusc has limited or no overlap.

fasciculate where the radial ornament of a shell is arranged in bundles.

fascioles tracts or bands of modified spines on sea urchins, or at the base of a gastropod.

filter-feeder feeding on plankton and organic matter that is filtered from sea water.

foraminifera single-celled animals with a calcite, aragonite or granular test (exterior) and a prominent foramen (aperture).

gastropod mollusc of the class Gastropoda; includes snails and slugs.

geniculation abrupt and persistent change in direction of valve growth.

glabella the head segment of a trilobite.

globose rounded as in globular or spherical.

impunctate lacking punctae.

inequilateral where the shell is asymmetrical, especially in bivalves.

inequivalve bivalve body plan where the two valves are different in shape and/or size.

infaunal living within a substrate, usually sedimentary, but can be a shell or wood substrate.

inflation a measure of how much room is available when the valves of a shell are shut, or of the surface curvature of a gastropod.

intercalating describes radial ornament that appears to arise between existing radials.

lanceolate elongate.

lirae fine thread-like shelly ornament.

lunule a natural moon-shaped depression that forms below the beaks of many bivalves.

Ma (abbreviation) millions of years ago.

macrofossils fossils that are easily seen with the naked eye.

microfossils fossils that are so small they can only be observed with a microscope.

nodose with ornament of prominent shelly knobs or spikes.

obovate leaf shape especially for angiosperms, broadest towards apex of leaf.

pedicle a muscular stalk in brachiopods that enables attachment to a substrate.

pinna (pl. pinnae) subdivision of a fern frond.

pinnate describes leaf arrangement; leaflets or pinnae arranged along a common axis.

planulate flat disc-shaped, especially in ammonoids.

plicae folds; another word for radial ornament especially in brachiopods.

punctae tiny pores or tubes within some brachiopod shells.

punctate bearing punctae.

pygidium the tail segment of a trilobite.

rachis main stem especially in ferns.

rastellum a comb-like structure developed along the hinge-line of some brachiopods.

resilifer a natural depression within the hinge-line of a bivalve shell occupied by the ligament.

rhabdosome the skeleton of a graptolite colony.

selenizone a band of shell developed in gastropods, formed by a prominent slit in the lip.

septae shelly wall structures developed in corals and cephalopod molluscs.

serpenticone coiled like a snake or tube as in some gastropods and cephalopods.

sessile attached to a substrate; not mobile.

sinus a natural groove or channel especially within gastropods.

spinose bearing spines.

stipe a major branch within a graptolite.

substrate the material upon which or within which an organism is attached.

sulcus a valley-shaped fold developed especially in brachiopod shells.

suture pattern formed at the intersection of the cephalopod chamber wall and venter.

theca an individual tube in a graptolite colony.

trace fossil a fossil produced by animal or plant behaviour; not a body fossil.

turbiniform resembling a turban in shape.

type species the species upon which the genus is defined and described.

umbilicus a depression formed at the centre of spiral growth in gastropod and cephalopod shells.

umbo (pl. umbones) the apical or earliest formed portion of a brachiopod valve containing the beak.

valve the name given to each of the two 'shells' of either a brachiopod or a bivalve mollusc.

venter the outermost rounded part of a coiled cephalopod.

whorl the shell developed in one full circle especially in cephalopods and gastropods.

Further reading

Beu, A.G., Maxwell, P.A. & Brazier, R. 1990. *Cenozoic Mollusca of New Zealand*. New Zealand Geological Survey Paleontological Bulletin 58. This book is now out of print but an electronic version can be downloaded from: www.gns.cri.nz

Bradshaw, M.A. 1999. Lower Devonian bivalves from the Reefton Group, New Zealand. Association of Australasian Palaeontologists, Memoir 20. 171 pp.

Cameron, E., Hayward, B. & Murdoch, G.A. 2008. *A Field Guide to Auckland: exploring the region's natural and historic heritage*. Godwit, Random House, Auckland. 304 pp.

Campbell, H.J. & Hutching, G. 2011 (revised edition). *In Search of Ancient New Zealand*. Penguin Books, Auckland. 240 pp.

Crampton, J.S. & Terezow, M.G. 2010. *The Kiwi Fossil Hunter's Handbook*. Random House, Auckland. 208 pp.

Darby, J., Fordyce, R.E., Mark, A., Probert, K. & Townsend, C. (editors) 2003. *The Natural History of Southern New Zealand*. University of Otago Press, Dunedin. 388 pp.

GNS Science QMap Series 1996–2011. Twenty-one 1:250,000 scale geological maps and accompanying illustrated booklets covering New Zealand. Available from GNS Science, Lower Hutt.

Gordon, D.P. (editor) 2009–12. *New Zealand Inventory of Biodiversity. Volume 1: Kingdom Animalia: Radiata, Lophotrochozoa, Deuterostomia. Volume 2: Animalia: Chaetognatha, Echdysozoa, Ichnofossils. Volume 3: Kingdoms Bacteria, Protozoa, Chromista, Plantae, Fungi*. Canterbury Univeristy Press, Christchurch.

Hollis, C.J., Beu, A.G., Crampton, J.S., Crundwell, M.P., Morgans, H.E.G., Raine, J.I., Jones, C.M. & Boyes, A.F. 2010. Calibration of the New Zealand Cretaceous–Cenozoic timescale to GTS2004. *GNS Science Report*, 2010/43. 20 pp.

Homer, L. & Moore, P.R. 1989. *Reading the Rocks: a guide to the geological features of the Wairarapa coast*. Landscape Publications, Wellington. 64 pp.

Marwick, J. 1953. *Divisions and Faunas of the Hokonui System (Triassic-Jurassic)*. New Zealand Geological Survey Paleontological Bulletin 21.

Morley, M.S. & Anderson, I. 2004. *A Photographic Guide to Seashells of New Zealand*. New Holland Publishers (NZ) Ltd., Auckland. 144 pp.

Thornton, J. 2003. *The Reed Field Guide to New Zealand Geology: an introduction to rocks, minerals and fossils*. Reed Books, Auckland. 276 pp.

GNS Science and its predecessors have produced a large number of relevant publications over the years and in particular paleontological monographs on specific fossil groups. These are available and can be ordered via the website: www.gns.cri.nz/Home/Products/Publications

Web resources

GNS Science: www.gns.cri.nz
Otago University: www.otago.ac.nz/geology/research/paleontology/
index.html
The Curio Bay Natural Heritage Centre: http://curiobay.org
The University of California Museum of Paleontology: http://
evolution.berkeley.edu
The Paleontology Portal: www.paleoportal.org
The Paleobiology Database: www.paleodb.org

Acknowledgements

The authors acknowledge the support of our GNS Science colleagues and in particular the following: Greg Browne, Philip Carthew, Roger Cooper, Giuseppe Cortese, Erica Crouch, Martin Crundwell, Des Darby, Kevin Faure, Sonja Fry, Chris Hollis, Carolyn Hume, Denise Kulhanek, Richard Levy, Margaret Low, Randall McDonnell, Dallas Mildenhall, Hugh Morgans, Joe Prebble, Ian Raine, Lucia Roncaglia, Poul Schioler, George Scott, John Simes, Graeme Stevens, Percy Strong, Julian Thomson, Roger Tremain and Marcus Vandergoes. We are also grateful for the constructive comments from our reviewers, Ian Ladds and Ian Raine. We acknowledge action shots 'in the field' of Luca Crampton (p. 6), and Daphne Lee and Michael Griffin (p. 25) collecting fossils.

Lastly, we acknowledge the stars of this book: the fossils. All examples illustrated herein are kept within the National Paleontology Collection (a research collection) at GNS Science, Avalon, Lower Hutt.

Image credits

Hamish Campbell: p. 25
Roger Cooper: p. 26
James Crampton: p. 6
Lloyd Homer: p. 32 (top and middle)
Carolyn Hume: graphic p. 8
Bill Lindqvist: p. 24 (bottom)
Marianna Terezow: all images, unless otherwise attributed

Index

Geological timescale

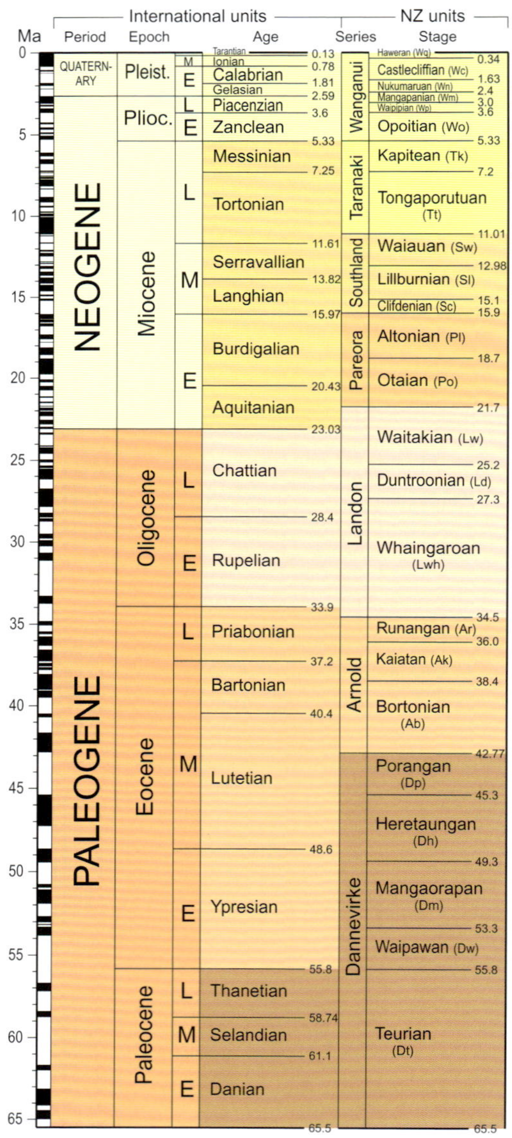

138

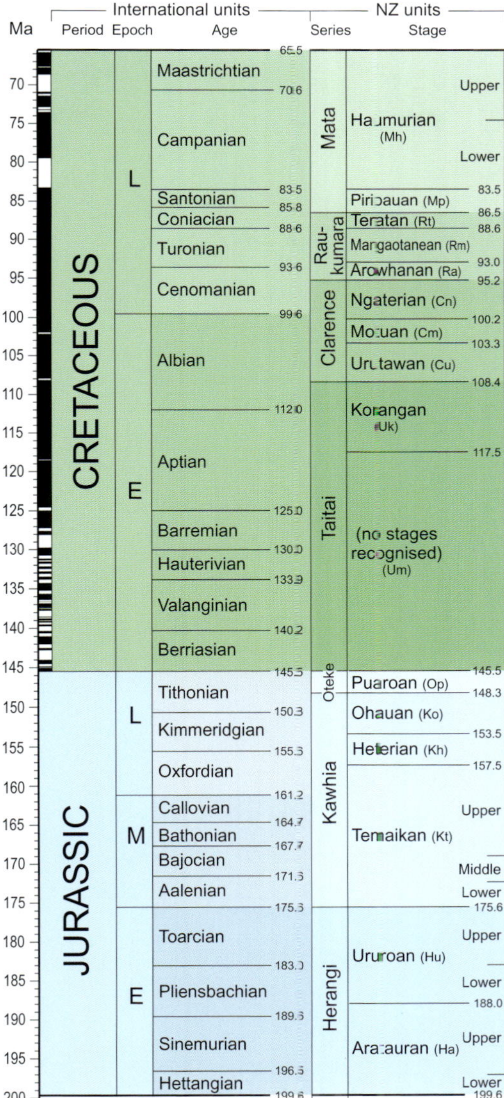
International units
NZ units
Ma
Period
Epoch
Age
Series
Stage
65.5
Maastrichtian
70.6
Upper
Campanian
Mata
Haumurian
(Mh)
Lower
L
83.5
83.5
Santonian
Piripauan (Mp)
85.8
86.5
Coniacian
Teratan (Rt)
88.6
88.6
Rau-
Turonian
kumara
Mangaotanean (Rm)
93.6
93.0
Arowhanan (Ra)
Cenomanian
95.2
Ngaterian (Cn)
Clarence
99.6
100.2
Motuan (Cm)
103.3
Albian
Urutawan (Cu)
108.4
112.0
Korangan
(Uk)
Aptian
117.5
E
Taitai
125.0
Barremian
(no stages
130.0
recognised)
Hauterivian
(Um)
133.9
Valanginian
140.2
Berriasian
145.5
145.5
Oteke
Puaroan (Op)
148.3
Tithonian
L
150.3
Ohauan (Ko)
Kimmeridgian
153.5
155.3
Heterian (Kh)
Oxfordian
Kawhia
157.5
161.2
Callovian
Upper
164.7
M
Bathonian
Temaikan (Kt)
167.7
Bajocian
171.6
Middle
Aalenian
Lower
175.3
175.6
Toarcian
Upper
Ururoan (Hu)
183.0
Lower
E
Pliensbachian
188.0
189.6
Herangi
Upper
Sinemurian
Aratauran (Ha)
196.5
Lower
Hettangian
199.6
199.6

CRETACEOUS
JURASSIC

Ma	International units			NZ units	
	Period	Epoch	Age	Series	Stage
199.6	TRIASSIC	L	Rhaetian	Balfour	Otapirian (Bo)
203.6			Norian		Warepan (Bw)
204.6					
212.0					Otamitan (Bm)
216.5			Carnian		Oretian (Br)
217.0					
227.5					
228.7		M	Ladinian	Gore	Kaihikuan (Gk)
237.0			Anisian		Etalian (Ge)
238.5					Malakovian (Gm)
244.5					
245.5		E	Olenekian		Nelsonian (Gn)
245.9			Induan		
249.5					
250.4					
251.0	PERMIAN	L	Changhsingian	'D'ur-ville'	'Makarewan' (YDm)
252.0					'Waiitian' (YDw)
253.8			Wuchiapingian		'Puruhauan' (YDp)
260.4		M	Capitanian	Aparima	Flettian (YAf)
265.8			Wordian		
266.5					Barettian (YAr)
268.0			Roadian		
270.6			Kungurian		Mangapirian (YAm)
273.0					
275.6			Artinskian		Telfordian (YAt)
280.0					
283.0					pre-Telfordian (Ypt)
284.4		E	Sakmarian		
294.6			Asselian		
299.0	CARBONIFEROUS	Pennsyl-vanian	Gzhelian		No stages recognised (F)
303.4			Kasimovian		
307.2			Moscovian		
311.7			Bashkirian		
318.1		Mississippian	Serpukhovian		
328.3			Visean		
345.3			Tournasian		
359.2	DEVONIAN	L	Famennian	Late	Famennian (JU)
374.5			Frasnian		Frasnian (JU)
385.3		M	Givetian	Middle	Givetian (JM)
391.8			Eifelian		Eifelian (JM)
397.5		E	Emsian	Early	Emsian (Jem)
407.0			Pragian		Pragian (Jpr)
411.2			Lochkovian		Lochkovian (Jlo)
416.0					

Ma	— International units —				— NZ units —	
	Period	Epoch	Age/Stage		Series	Stage

International units (boundary ages in Ma)

Period	Epoch	Age/Stage	Base (Ma)
SILURIAN	Pridol		418.7
SILURIAN	Lud.	Ludfordian	421.3
SILURIAN	Lud.	Gorstian	422.9
SILURIAN	Wen.	Homerian	426.2
SILURIAN	Wen.	Sheinwoodian	428.2
SILURIAN	Llandovery	Telychian	436.0
SILURIAN	Llandovery	Aeronian	439.0
SILURIAN	Llandovery	Rhuddanian	443.7
ORDOVICIAN	L	Hirnantian	445.6
ORDOVICIAN	L	Katian	455.8
ORDOVICIAN	L	Sandbian	460.9
ORDOVICIAN	M	Darriwilan	466.1
ORDOVICIAN	M	Dapingian	471.8
ORDOVICIAN	E	Floian	478.6
ORDOVICIAN	E	Tremadocian	488.3
CAMBRIAN	Furongian	Stage 10	492.0
CAMBRIAN	Furongian	Stage 9	496.0
CAMBRIAN	Furongian	Paibian	499.0
CAMBRIAN	Series 3	Guzhangian	503.0
CAMBRIAN	Series 3	Drumian	506.5
CAMBRIAN	Series 3	Stage 5	510.0
CAMBRIAN	Series 2	Stage 4	515.0
CAMBRIAN	Series 2	Stage 3	542

(Top of chart = 416.0 Ma)

NZ units (boundary ages in Ma)

Series	Stage	Base (Ma)
Pridol		416.0
Lud.	Ludfordian (Elu)	421.3
Lud.	Gorstian (Elu)	422.9
Wen.	Homerian (Ewe)	426.2
Wen.	Sheinwoodian	428.2
Llandovery	Telychian (Ela)	436.1
Llandovery	Aeronian (Ela)	439.0
Llandovery	Rhuddanian (Ela)	443.7
Late	Bolindian (Vbo)	450.19
Late	Eastonian (Vea)	455.8
Late	Gisbornian (Vgi)	460.9
Middle	Darriwilian (Vda)	
Middle	Yapeenian (Vya)	468.1
Middle	Castlemain. (Vca)	468.84
Middle		471.8
Early	Chewtonian (Vch)	473.5
Early	Bendigonian (Vbe)	476.33
Early	Lancefieldian (Vla)	487.0
Early	Warendian (Vla)	488.3
Furongian	Datsonian (Xda)	489.52
Furongian	Payntonian (Xpa)	492.0
Furongian	Iverian (Xiv)	496.0
Furongian	Idamean (Xid)	499.0
Middle	Mindyallan (Xmi)	501.04
Middle	Boomerangian (Xbo)	503.0
Middle	Undillan (Xun)	504.93
Middle	Floran (Xfl)	506.2
Middle	Templeton (Xor)	509.04
Middle	Ordian (Xor)	513.5
Early	No stages recognised (XL)	542

141

Notes

Notes